INNER MARATHON
The Diary of a Jogging Nun

*with love
and a blessing
Joan Sauro*

The masked bandit jogs again, through the cold and broken streets of the parish, saying the Jesus Prayer, stealing the people, unaware.

INNER MARATHON
The Diary of a Jogging Nun

Joan Sauro, C.S.J.

PAULIST PRESS
New York/Ramsey

Library of Congress Catalog Card Number: 81-84385

ISBN: 0-8091-2441-6

Published by Paulist Press
545 Island Road, Ramsey, N.J. 07446

Printed and bound in the United States of America

to
Janet

year one

So I started jogging. Mostly to keep body and soul together.

Actually, I have been running all my life. In the family album there is a picture of me in diapers with my left arm in a sling. Big tears are rolling down. I had been running in my aunt's house and slipped on the high gloss. At picnics, I always won the foot races, for girls under six, for girls six to twelve, for unmarried women. By that time I was running on a tennis court, swinging unorthodox strokes, winning only because my legs were faster. I ran from a potential rapist. I ran when the snowball I threw entered the open window of a delivery truck and struck the driver. Then I entered the convent.

One day another novice looked at me with affection. I ran. In habit and old ladies' shoes I ran, faster than at any picnic or tennis court. I ran circles around the old seminary where we all lived, round and round that high towered, austere, stone fortress, like Achilles running around Troy, spending his anger. I didn't know what I was spending.

When I wasn't running, I was kneeling safely in the chapel, kneeling in the stone fortress on strong runner's legs. I knelt for hours without visible support. One Holy Thursday in the middle of the kneeling I became conscious of my breathing, and conscious that a word was being said in the inhale-exhale. The word was "Jesus." I took it for a blessing on my running and kneeling.

A long time after, I am learning to stand and face certain things. This diary is one of those things.

In the old days we used to read the lives of the saints, the better to emulate their outsized virtues. Today it seems appropriate to read the lives of one another. It is in this spirit that I give you my story, that you may be encouraged to tell yours.

February 14. It may have all started with Sister Consilia, my sixth grade teacher, although until last week I had scarcely a clue. She spied me, this Sister Consilia now past eighty, in the mother house dining room, fixed me with frozen eye and bony finger and "Do you say the prayers I taught you do you Jesus meek and humble of heart make my heart like unto thine O most sacred heart of Jesus I place all my trust in thee sweet heart of Jesus be my love sweet heart of Mary be my salvation?"

Well no, I don't. But something like it. Somehow it all contracted to "Jesus," or maybe that's all I heard you say, and I don't even know for sure it all started with you, but chances seem good it may have.

Later I met the Russian Pilgrim, but by then the prayer had long since made its way to my heart.

He was a marathoner, this Russian Pilgrim, doing his forty-three or four miles a day with his Bible in one breast pocket and his *Philokalia* in the other. In his heart he carried the wish to pray always and the Jesus Prayer the holy staret taught him to say on his rosary beads. The thumb on the Pilgrim's left hand was worn thin from sliding over twelve thousand beads a day.

Twelve thousand times a day he prayed, "Lord Jesus Christ, have mercy on me," until in no time at all the prayer slipped from his lips down into his heart and started saying itself to the tune of his heartbeat.

Soon his eyes followed suit and dropped down to his heart too, into those many and convoluted chambers where the Jesus Prayer was going on like a broken record and the Jesus of the Prayer started showing him little by little the mystery of his sensuous and spiritual heart. Then the marathon really began, forty-three or four miles a day through the labyrinthine ways of that heart. All the while, the Pilgrim was breathing in on "Lord Jesus Christ," and breathing out on "have mercy on me."

And that is just about where I am now, at the gateway to the convoluted heart, taking two steps and a breath in on "Je" and two steps and a breath out on "sus."

February 15. My feet take me through the broken streets of an unpresuming, hybrid parish called St. Brigid and St. Joseph. The first steps are all downhill, from home to Twin Trees Too Restaurant, where I take a left on ice and skid past Jenny Herron's dress shop where the mannequins pose in lightless windows. Jenny sits in furs at the Saturday night liturgy. Jenny has no idea I send Jesus into her shop every morning. The block ends at the Twin Trees pizza barn where fresh bread is baking and I remember Jesus blessing the loaves and breaking them. I hear him say, "No one is to have the whole loaf. Of you."

Then the long, seemingly endless, one-half mile up Willis Avenue hill, dotted with dogs and little children, past the school and church and convent up near the top, and the Congregational church, abandoned save for birds in the bell tower. A left on Genesee and my legs rest on a down hill toward the DeSantis music house on the left and the old homestead of my dead music teacher on the right. Jesus, have mercy on her.

The United Methodist church is followed by Beebe the dentist, Edward J. Ryan and Son Funeral Home and the policewoman with the leathered face, frozen in every season. I bless her, the librarians in the Hazard Branch and whoever is pulling the bells in the Episcopalian church. I wave to Red Ertinger, pumping Mobil on weekdays, passing the collection basket on weekends. Cookie Caloia at the car wash is marshaling a line of cars headed by Ed Ryan in the hearse.

A sharp left on ice at the Key Bank leads to the Tops Market on the right, and a long strip of interesting shops on the left—everything from TV's and fleas, to upholstery, Jocko's Shebeen and the American Legion Tipperary Hill Post 1361. It all ends at the Casual Inn. I take a quick left up heartbreak hill where Dick Allen is loading the truck at the auction house, and a quick right past Kerstetter cabinetmakers. For one long level mile I sprint on Emerson Avenue, past the Lipe-Rollway Factory where a woman calls 691

3

over the roar and violent scream of machines.

A sudden clump of trees hides a small dump and a red cardinal. With one steep climb, I am home with cleaner heart and well-oiled limbs.

February 18. Run easy. Thoughtless. Gentle. Jesus. The road seems to lower kindly and the sun pull me up on a string, up toward home. They say that when Edward Villella dances the prodigal son, he moves as if pulled on a string toward his father.

February 19. Below zero every day. It is difficult to protect my hands, so I open and close them, in rhythm, until hands, feet, breath and prayer are synchronized in open-close, left-right, in-out, Je-sus.

There's a ragtag, one-woman band playing on the slopes and slides of this parish.

February 24. Dry as a cold bone, so I jog up the middle of the Willis Avenue hill, past Mom and Dad's green car, parked in front of the church. They are in at the 10 o'clock Mass. I feel better, seeing their car and knowing where they are, as if they were the children and I the parent.

February 27. Grey to black day, sunless, dogless, practically carless, unobtrusive Wednesday, in the middle of the week like a sandwich.

February 28. Three to five inches fell in the night, got run over and half-plowed. Now there are two to three inches of moist brown sugar underfoot in the street, twisting my ankles unmercifully.

I want you to know my aim is high, and as soon as this wind dies down,
I'm up and out for keeps. That's why I practice these trash can leaps.

My brother asks me why I don't stay home in winter and run in place. I tell him I would not persevere. Once I got a side ache or lost my breath, I would quit. I run outdoors to put myself *out* of place, far from home, so that when a pain comes, I cannot stop. At that point I'm halfway out, with no choice but to run home.

I think I put myself in this apartment with Janet for the same reason. I put myself *out* of place, out of convent, so that when I want to ease off I cannot. I am forced to live responsibly and to depend on others. It is a kind of situation ethics.

March 3.

> there are cardinals all over the place—
> or maybe the same one
>
> the grape ivy, upright till now,
> has thrown itself out the window
> with longing for the sun

March 5. Steady rain at 8. By 8:45 it turns half rain half snow. Not so wet except for the feet.

I say the Jesus Prayer slowly, trying to forget everything else, praying his name to wash me like baptism.

The run is like the weather, half and half.

March 12. It is the same driving wind that belts us with snow today that last Monday poured down rain. In between came sun and 60°.

March simulates all seasons, serves them all up in smorgasbord fashion. Only the houseplants know. Sure of themselves, they slowly unfurl, one shiny new leaf, then another. Plants know spring has nothing to do with the elements. Spring is a quality of light. So is heaven.

6

March 15. Heaven is cleaning house today, throws down buckets of dirty wash and a fistful of snow on runners. The wind is a roaring vacuum cleaner, cleaning heaven, dumping bagfuls of dirt, paper, cans, a yellow lampshade to leap over and an old man.

I watch him, the old man, slug down the dirt green side of his house, turn back, turn forward, turn back toward the wrong house where he is banged in shut by a loose door. A car rolls slowly up to the house, rolls back, rolls up, rolls out the driver, unsure which house is his. None of them are.

March 20. Winter went for good today and took the ice and snow handicap with it. We still have the wind.

March 21. Every day, before I run, I sit as prayerfully as I can and read a Gospel story, for an hour or so. For twenty years I have been turning these pages faithfully, reading God's story. Today I wonder. Does God read my story?

The answer comes out on the road, somewhere in the windy stretch up Willis Avenue. I see a picture of an ageless Jesus, with wire glasses fallen down his nose. He is sitting in profile, in a Rembrandt lighting—dark brown background, warm gold light on his face.

A book is opened on his lap and he is reading, thoroughly engrossed. Now and again he smiles, gets excited, lifts his head up to relish some passage, turns the page slowly, sighs, cries, shifts nervously in his chair, laughs uproariously at an illustration.

There are many, many books of stories on the darkened shelves behind him, but today he is reading my story, and loving it, as each person hopes.

April 6. I hem and haw at the weather, would rather run in snow, ice, sleet, rain, scorching sun, anything than in wind.

7

Today it comes at me in sixty mile an hour gusts. Today I learn a lesson from the wind:

It is not always possible to go forward.
It is always possible to go up and down.

April 7. My greatest joy in jogging is when my two feet are in the air.

High or low—there's not a place I won't go. But I want you to know my aim is high, and as soon as this wind dies down, I'm up and out for keeps. That's why I practice these trash can leaps.

April 10. The wind is still furious. All night long it banged the windows, shook the house and even the chairs we sat in for prayer this morning.

A child is playing the piano in the DeSantis music house. One small finger exercise, played to the beat of the metronome, comes through the bay window and rides on the wind to me, jogging by in 4/4 time, to the rhythm of Je - sus.

My legs are a metronome too. I slow them down or speed them up, to adjust to the wind. But I do not break the rhythm of my song.

Every athlete knows that the way to win the game is to control the rhythm.

April 15. Easter Sunday. Peter and John start out on their way toward the tomb. They run side by side most of the way. Then John outruns Peter and reaches the tomb first. He sees and believes.

John, patron saint of joggers, saves his kick for the end. Poets always get there first and have to wait for the Peters, the rocks of the world, to catch up.

April 17. I hear the ground breaking as I run by.

> a bulb breaks ground soundlessly,
> all at once greenly
>
> no bells peal,
> not a note
> for valor in the field

April 23. Run under a canopy of soft green fuzz, green puff-balls exploding, colored balloons, and the parish is a circus. Every dog is out doing his act. I need steel guards on my legs. I need a warden. I need the hound of heaven, chasing me down the nights and down the days, catching me in the labyrinthine ways of my own mind.

April 24. Far away in the heart of the forest, the contemplative nun at Still Point House of Prayer sits in the yoga position. She breathes the Jesus Prayer gently, in and out, Jesus, Son of David, have mercy on us. Then all the nuns chant the prayer together, there mid the murmuring pines and bird song.

Here in the heart of the city, the active nun jogs the broken streets of the parish, breathing the same name of Jesus, gently, in stride, two steps to a syllable, Je - sus, up and down the hills, into the dusty gutters, around parked cars, mid honks and beeps of passers-by, some friendly, some frisky, the name of Jesus breathed on them all.

April 26. All the windows on the way are thrown open to spring. At the Lipe-Rollway Factory the machines scream violently through every window. I stretch out my arms and open my hands all the long length of the factory. Jesus, have

A child is playing the piano in the DeSantis music house. One small
finger exercise, played to the beat of the metronome, comes through the
bay window and rides on the wind to me, jogging by in $4/4$ time, to the
rhythm of Je—sus.

mercy on all who work in violence. Protect their hands and eyes and souls.

April 27. Just a little more gentle jogging today, just a little more quiet in praying. Jesus, Son of David, have mercy on her. Chrissy Susnock was hit by a school bus this morning, less than an hour ago, in the street below our apartment window.

Just a little irritated with the speed and screech sounds in the street, I had slammed the porch door shut and tried to attend to the Morning Praise we were saying. Then there came a screech and scream more terrible than the rest. From the porch we could see—Chrissy lay face down in the middle of the street, in between the garbage truck and the head-start school bus. Her face was a mass of purple.

We called Father Libera and went down to the street. The neighbors were making her as comfortable as they could, with pillows and blankets off their unmade beds. Two black men from the garbage truck took up detail at either end of the street, flagging away traffic. One's face was on the other side of the city, looking for his own children, wondering if they made it to school safely.

Just in from the night shift, the child's father came stumbling out of bed and onto the street. The ambulance came, followed by the police. They iced her face and put splints on her arms. The priest talked gently to her. The mother, having raced back from work, tore from the car and shook all the way to the spot where her child lay. She knelt down and buried her face in the disfigured one.

"Take me home, Mommy."

"Get up. They've got to put her in the ambulance." The mother did not move.

"*You* have to go with her in the ambulance." This came from a stalwart neighbor who knew the right approach, to motherly duty. She and the father pulled up the mother, still shaking, who then hugged the teenage daughter who should

11

have been minding her sister and said, "It's not your fault, honey."

After they left, there were only two white pieces of paper blowing in the street, two empty bandage bags to say this morning at 7:50 a child was hit by a bus, here on our street, and her life was spared, maybe because two nuns were praying, however badly, in a noisy room above the street.

May 1. First week in May is 40°. I run with black gloves on, past the blooming magnolia which has more trust than I. The tree stands in a cold trance, unable to go back to bud or forth to full bloom. I wave a black hand to a pink tree.

May 2. At the gynecologist's I wait, sitting on a table top, in gown and socks. After a while I notice a strange thing going on with my legs.

My right leg dangles down from the table, is still, like a heavy anchor, knows very well I should be here for the periodic checkup.

My left leg swings back and forth furiously, rhythmically, saying the Jesus Prayer, saying let's get out of here.

After the examination, I jump for relief off the table and jog the three miles home.

May 12. Last night it was 90°, so we sat out the heat on the front porch. At midnight the Allied Chemical whistle blew, and a jogger in trunks went by with his dog. The man's feet splat splat on the hot sidewalk.

At 7 A.M. it was only 10° cooler. Two girl friends jogged together in the street.

At 8 I am on the road, skipping over the purple trash bags the gay grocer carried out. I say the Jesus Prayer slowly, up the hot Willis Avenue hill, down the Genesee strip, and slow down in front of Ryan's Funeral Home to pray Jesus,

Son of David, have mercy on James, lying skin and bones in the death house. James Tierney, father of Sister Patricia and Sister Marguerite. They're home eating breakfast now, so I keep watch with running feet.

James is risen. He is not here. Hurry, feet, hurry to proclaim it to the two sisters, feet pounding the sidewalk, beating the name of Jesus over and over into the streets and sidewalks. Long after I'm gone the name of Jesus will stay engraved in the cement, beaten in by rubber cleats.

When I get home, I take my shoes off and find maple seeds lodged between the cleats, sprouting there.

May 14.

> There were ten white pennywafers
> on the paten this morning.
> I ate one in hope. When I die,
> put a white penny in each eye.

May 21. A run in a hot wind, shirt flapping loose; so am I. The magnolia is deflowered now. Fresh new leaves, soft looking and green, make a beautiful ball of green out of the magnolia tree.

Nobody pays any attention. Twenty steps beyond, the bridal wreath is in full bloom.

May 30. In a strange town, in a strange house, my first thought is to find a jogging route. I don't have to look far—a large circular drive in front of Stella Maris Retreat House, where I am staying, and one city block outside the gates make a good quarter mile track.

The dogs are always with me. Two large, white plaster hunters, with their ribs in bold relief, guard the doorway. They have a lean and hungry look.

Because it is a strange route, I tend to run it over my regular route. Now I am at the Twin Trees pizza barn, now passing the school, now at the top of Genesee Street. I do the same thing with my life here, trying to wear the same old schedule and the same old familiar clothes. It always takes me a few days to leave the old ways and enjoy my stay in the new place.

June 1. After jogging, I go down to the lake to watch the rhythm of the tides, and the mindless way they repeat themselves, ebb and flow over a small rock formation, with no thought, no Jesus Prayer.

An old oak leaf, stained brown and crimson in last year's vintage, comes floating around my right side in the slow mechanical ride the tide makes. The leaf heads for the narrow strait between two large rocks. Having somehow managed the winter, the leaf has now to negotiate the narrow pass if it is to sail the wide sea. There is no alternative.

The tide rocks the leaf back and forth at the pass, back and forth endlessly, as I watch. The leaf's points are too wide to make the pass. The tide turns the leaf from side to side, but the leaf is helpless, cannot pull the points in, cannot suck itself together and slip through.

I think to pick the leaf up and lay it down on the other side of the rocks. I think to do this because it is what I wish God would do to me, lift me out of an impossible situation. The way the points keep banging the sides of the rock is frustrating, less to the leaf than to me, watching the visual enactment of my life.

One of these times, I think, the tide will come rising in a swift rush and lift the leaf tumultuously over the impasse. Then it's either drown or ride over the obstacle.

Meanwhile, I wonder if the leaf were flipped around, with its points backward, it could then squeeze through the narrow space. As I wonder, the tide does just that, spins the

14

leaf around, and with its stem leading the way, the leaf backs itself through the narrow strait and out to the wide sea.

I follow the leaf out of sight, wish it well, turn my head a little to the right and discover a motorboat in a dead float in the middle of the lake and a man waving two bright red flags at me.

I stand quickly, wave back, sprint up the hill and into town as fast as I can on a Jesus Prayer. I keep hearing Stevie Smith's poem over the Prayer:

> I was much too far out all my life
> And not waving but drowning.

June 2.

> The great heart of the house heaves
> lower parts to passion, through cool upper rooms
> hums and pumps its basement burn.
> I school myself at every turn.
>
> Next to fire and unfired by it
> lies cold storage, preserver by chill,
> humming its will in cold concern.
> There is a lesson here to learn.
>
> Outside walls are cold to touch,
> spurn the blaze for which they yearn.
> I swing the windows eastern wide
> but school myself at every turn.
>
> Running the quarter mile track
> is all for distance, as walls are.
> From linear to circular pattern.
> There is a lesson here to learn.
> I school myself at every turn.

June 3. Pentecost. I run the prayer wheel in twenty mindless laps, like the sea tides. I run like a ball of fire, on wheels of a fiery chariot.

June 13. Back home bread dough from the pizza barn is baking, throwing its fresh smell all over the street as I jog by. Take my body for bread. Take my blood for your life. I tear out a handful and throw it for bread to the breadmakers, throw handfuls of snowy white bread through the open school windows to rain down on the children singing in there. Take my life's blood with you, lady with the golden hair at the bus stop. Take my life's blood, you pumpers of gas at the Mobil Station, my life's energy for free, long-lasting, not like the high-priced gas you pump. Throw handfuls of the bread of myself all along the way I jog, fling in a wide arch the living bread into the Tops Market where the baker slowly rises from his morning coffee to start his bread. Through the windows of the Lipe-Rollway Factory, bread and wine for an early lunch break. Body and Blood of Jesus, body and blood of me.

June 30. Wet wind, hot air, grey morning.

Before I know it, I leap over the wings of a dead bird, mashed into the sidewalk, and, in the leaping, frighten a baby rabbit. He makes for a bush on legs faster than mine will ever be. The block ends at Ryan's Funeral Home where the hearse is parked across the sidewalk, ready to lead the parade with flags and lights. I sidestep the hearse on nimble feet.

My mind is not so nimble. I cannot put together this death, life, death—all found so close together in one city block. I can only see them separately, one after the other, like my steps.

Soon that is all I hear, my Jesus steps, pounding the concrete for an answer, or at least for some sense of wholeness.

July 9. Back at Stella Maris Retreat House and the quarter mile track, three fourths in holy ground, one fourth out in the world. Sister Fridolin, in full habit, is walking the track slowly, walking for a constitutional. Her fingers walk the track of her rosary beads. I overtake her on the first lap, pick her up—she is tiny, under five feet—and we give the kiss of peace in mid air.

Not a great deal of difference between us, Sister Fridolin. Your rosary beads are my Jesus Prayer.

Mama John, in modified habit, leads the vacuum cleaner out onto the front porch and warns me as I pass that I shall be dead before I am fifty. I trail, "Oh no," in the wind after me. In a flower box lay me to rest. Flowers will spring from my chest.

July 10. In the middle of our prayer wheel, Mary stands in a bed of flowers with her hands folded. Mary's story is all in her feet.

Her right foot stands flat on the ground, trailing vines and roses. But her left foot, ah, that is swung behind her right foot and lifted up, on toes. Mary is running a track of her own, and swiftly, as is evident in the wind-blown sweep of her clothes on that left side.

This is not Stella Maris, star of the sea, as everyone thinks. This is Mary running into the hill country to see dear Elizabeth.

July 12. Jesus Christ within us, around, above, under and among us. Jesus Christ unseen, lovingly between.

August 1. I jog the prayer wheel as usual, saying my Jesus Prayer as usual. On my way into the house, a young man on retreat catches my ear, catches my ear for forty-five minutes.

As I head for the kitchen and breakfast, his mother

17

catches my other ear. She is seated in the large cannonball furniture. She is a very large woman, with soft rolls running down her front, and three or four soft rolled chins. She tells me about her son, whom I had just left out on the balcony. She tells me about her grandchildren back home, about her life with them all, and about the life she had dreamed of having.

I listen as long as I can, trying to concentrate on her face. But I am much distracted, and the last conscious thought I have as I look into the soft rolls is, "Your eyes are so close together."

Then I hear the words, "Jesus is the Fat Lady."

I can't say that I had been thinking about J.D. Salinger and Franny and Zooey. I certainly wasn't thinking about that part where Seymour tells his brother and sister to look out into the audience and find the Fat Lady. Then, be funny for her. Have your shoes shined for her, because the Fat Lady is Christ himself.

I hadn't been thinking about any of this as I jogged the prayer wheel, saying my Jesus Prayer. But now all the Fat Ladies I left back home shuffle across my eyes.

Later I look to see what else Franny and Zooey have to say.

When you say the Jesus Prayer, Zooey tells Franny, say the prayer to Jesus, as he is, and not as you wish he would be (169). He is the Son of God who said that a human being, any human being, is more valuable to God than anything else on the face of the earth (165).

And "if it's the religious life you want, you ought to know right now that you're missing out on every single goddam religious action that's going on around this house. You don't even have sense enough to *drink* when somebody brings you a cup of consecrated chicken soup—which is the only kind of chicken soup Bessie [their mother] ever brings to anybody.

"Even if you went out and searched the whole world for

a master—some guru, some holy man—to tell you how to say your Jesus Prayer properly, what good would it do you? How in *hell* are you going to recognize a legitimate holy man when you see one if you don't even know a cup of consecrated chicken soup when it's right in front of your nose?" (196).

August 6.

> transfigured world
>
> to render the landscape abstract
> reduce the view
> to a few horizontal lines
> and well defined spaces
>
> a thalo curve, earth green bar,
> sky ultra marine.
> Run three fourths up your eyeballs green,
> top quarter blue.

August 12. Farewell, people of Stella Maris. What can I give you for thanks? Only my poor feet all over the place. This is my body, given for you. This is my blood, running around in circles for you.

August 22. At Oberlin College for a clown ministry workshop. The place swelters in the heat and the 95% humidity. I am stripped to shirt, shorts and shoes, but still my legs lift like lead around the long quadrangle of buildings. I angle off to another long quad around a burnt grass park. Graffiti decorates the sidewalks around Oberlin College. I pound a hot Jesus Prayer into the graffiti and do the burnt grass quad a second and third time, writing JESUS over the words.

A sudden rain comes pouring down to wash me and the graffiti.

August 24. Every day I jog my two and a half miles merrily, thinking that this must surely put me in with the relatively fit half of humanity.

Not so. This I see in pantomime class, where 99% of my body refuses to bend, swing, pivot, lift, roll, or stay in place. Jogging is the only thing I have done for my body, thus far.

August 26. The last picture I have of Oberlin College is of Reid Gilbert, on stage in his black and white costume, doing his impeccable pantomimes, after the manner of Marcel Marceau.

Reid Gilbert stands like a poor man on stage, with only his body to tell us his stories. No props, no scenery, no color, no sound—we may as well all be deaf and dumb. Reid Gilbert is reduced in his black and white costume to a black and white photograph, to a series of black and white photographs. In turn he is an inept surgeon, sculptor, maskmaker, schoolboy, human being. All of his apples have worms in them. He loses every tug of war, steps on every stray wad of gum. But we stand up, yell "bravo" and batter our hands red for him who shows us how poor we are before God, and how lovable.

Today I jog with a black and white picture of Reid Gilbert in my eyes, until I see a man raking his lawn on Emerson Avenue. I do not see the rake, only the long pulling movement of the man's body.

September 5. Today we bury my Uncle Paul, so I jog the Jesus Prayer for him. Some of the prayer and some of the poor runner-scarcely-clad hangs on me as I enter the sad silence of the death room. "I came in naked and I will go out naked."

Between me standing here and you, Paul, inches away in a casket, is the biggest leap I shall ever make. Only the name of Jesus will be bridge enough over the long darkness.

Uncle Paul's gold wedding band shines on the waxy fingers folded across his front. Aunt Mary shined it all of their life together, and one last loving time now.

I stand before the church doors with my Aunt Mary and dead uncle. The last time we all stood together in front of these church doors, I was in a pink gown and they were in wedding clothes.

When night comes, Janet and I help another family celebrate Mass in their home. A young child sleeps through it all, laid out flat on the couch with his small hands folded across his front. Someone remarks, "He should have a lily in his hands," and the circle closes, the gold band of love and death binding us all together.

September 15. I'm running in the last of the sun and I know it. All around I see more of change than I care to see.

The bent grass throws long, finger lake shadows across the sidewalk. There are beads of dew running down the grass stalks. These translucent, single-minded water lights (small as pinheads with hordes of angels dancing upon) throw long, dark shadows on the stalks.

Everything earthly throws a shadow, I suppose, even pure water crystals, crying their eyes out for our Lady of Sorrows.

September 20. I can only call him M., a handsome, gentle dude who finds himself with another woman. His wife is grateful for their beautiful children and the good years of marriage they had together. His wife is also profoundly angry, and distributes her anger indiscriminately.

I beat the anger into the sidewalk, hers and mine.

In the beginning of my religious life, I beat poor Body.
It was the religious style then—beat the lust out of the flesh.
There was no anger to beat. That came later.

Body is tough as nails now, jogging being a far more
healthy exercise. These legs carry me over miles, when my
poor, noble head is much distracted.

September 21.

Today I packed my heart
piece by worn piece
leaving you an old valise
with a prayer. No, today
I unpacked my heart
memento after memento
leaving you an old prayer
in an empty compartment.

September 24. Edward J. Ryan and Son stand in the parking lot of their Funeral Home as I jog by. Son, in a handsome dark suit, tips an imaginary hat and calls, "I take my
hat off to you, Sister. That's dedication."

"Good luck to you in the coming election," I shout
back, you handsome dude, standing with your father outside
the death house. One out of two marriages ends in divorce.

September 28. In the coming election I will run through
the broken streets of the parish with the name of Jesus written across my shirt.

And under the shirt an icon of Christ Savior tattooed on
my back, like the character in Flannery O'Connor's story.

The eyes of Christ do not look outward. Those piercing,

22

all demanding eyes look inward, making me transparent under the shirt with the name of Jesus on it.

September 30. Jogging in the grey wet morning is as close as I come to take nothing for the journey, neither walking staff nor traveling bag. No bread, no money, certainly not two jackets. Bless whomever you meet, going from place to place, and shake the dust off your shoes where you are not received. Spread the good news everywhere.

I am deep into these holy thoughts when Mrs. DeFabio, just dropped off from morning Mass, greets me with, "You looka so nica, Seesta. You gotta nica forma."

I finish the route in record time.

October 1. Sunless and wet. All the world is falling down on my head—chestnut falls, acorn leaves and halves of shells, the nuts and bolts of a world undone.

In the schoolroom two children shout out numbers, competing for speed and accuracy. Better to better your own time or style, I think.

A barroom stool holds the door ajar at Jocko's Shebeen. We're all airing our insides out today.

At the factory a woman's voice calls 197 over the PA, through the roar and ring of machines, the slow grind of nuts and bolts.

October 15.

Changing

First the veins go,
in a leaf, I mean.
Yellow through green,

23

blue through yellow
made blue green.
It seems reasonable
veins should change first,
bleeding grief into
the rest of the leaf.

October 17. There's a way of going up hills—slow and on tiptoe.

There's a way of coming down—unbound.

There's a way of bucking the breeze—imitate trees.

There's a way of holding the hands—in a loose curl, like the ocean rolling in on itself,

And a way of holding the shoulders—level, as if carrying chips. But don't. They're heavy.

There's a way of keeping the elbows and a way of keeping the heart. Unlocked.

There's a way of running in rain—the way of running in snow, sun and cloud. Faithfully.

October 31. Fartlek is a Swedish word meaning, "speed play."

Playing with speed, use all your body gears, from jogging to sprinting, fast or slow as you feel like moving. Fartlek is like free form skating. Like free verse poetry.

If you like goals and controls, you will not like fartlek. You will not like Halloween either.

November 3. There are twenty-seven million of us out here today. Some run blind, some pregnant. Some make love in their minds, some make peace. A father jogs by with a load of son on his back. I love you, Daddy of the big shoulders.

24

Mary is running a track of her own, and swiftly, running into the hill country to see dear Elizabeth.

I take a long, slow warm down, then kneel down to see water beads on the undersides of leaves. The beads cling to every spine. One large mirror magnifies the veins. Watery soul, magnify the Lord.

November 5. pray on empty. sing on empty. work on empty. run on empty, all the way home on empty.

November 14.

> birds croak
> dry in the throat
>
> trees croak
> dry in the bones
>
> indistinguishable tones

November 19. The ideal pace is the one you can maintain all the way. Even pace does not mean equal effort. It usually means holding back early and pushing late.

I'm pushing now, in the late of the year and the darkening of light. In vain I look for color. Oh, there may be a few red hawthorn berries, but the overall impression is grey and burnt umber. Earth and sky are mute and faded.

All the lights and people are indoors, flickering warmth through the windows, getting ready for a thanksgiving.

May we all run home in peace, into light unceasing.

November 28. Janet's birthday.

Grant-in-Aid

Enclosed
please find
your grant
to work in her
inner city.
We call to mind
this is a kind
of fellowship
you have won
in terms reciprocal
regarding
remuneration
and such.
This is no
pastoral park.
You're in the heart
of the city—
the naked
needy
core.
That is what a fellowship
is for.

December 4. My run is a cameo performance of my day, of my whole life. My unwhole life.

Jogging this route is better. There is a clear beginning, a long and varied middle, and a definite end, coming home. My life in miniature is whole, as my life in large is not. I long to be whole. Healed. Sealed like a snow world in a glass ball and lifted up to high heaven.

There are whole prayers offered to God, and there are broken ones.

27

December 25. 8:30 A.M., a balmy 55°. Jogging Christmas day is best of all. God is at his most imaginative, having dreamed the image of Jesus in the night. Candles are lightless in windows this black and wet Christmas. God's people are still dreaming. May you wake to each other's gifts and take them for love. Or at least for a step in love's direction.

All the broken families look doubly broken on Christmas. Some of my family are absent around my parents' table, having come two days ago, out of duty, out of guilt, out of a two way necessity, out of a half lit, well disguised hope.

December 27. Speed strains the body; distance trains it.

December 28. A long white wire strung across the broken sidewalk catches my left foot, catches like a hunter's snare, except the wire is loose and so comes riding up on my foot. Later I am amazed to read the psalm prayer for this day of Holy Innocents. Our soul has escaped, like a bird from the hunter's net.

The Gospel is for kings and kids.

Your coming to earth was a helpless coming. We need cunning to save our feet from the hunter's snare. The wise men had cunning and so found another way around Herod. The innocents were without cunning and found no way around. Unless, perhaps, there was a mother or two crafty enough to devise something like a wicker basket among reeds. If so, her innocent was saved that day. What a strange coming, when innocents need cunning.

December 29. Janet's kindergarten children play to Bach's *Shepherd's Pastorale.* She brought the record home, so I do seven minute stretch exercises to it.

A lovely, easy, rise and fall, like a breath, like a measured tumble.

28

Up and down situps, be my body's sweating adoration. Stretch, legs, like scissors in mid-air, cutting out gold stars there. Roll over. Push up from the floor and down. Up and down slowly, until lips kiss the floor of the earth of the manger bed.

Stretch for all you're worth, arms and legs and lips and soul. Sweating soul, stretch to make an open inn of yourself.

January 4. I'm going in circles around the mother house front, twenty-five times around like twenty-five silver dollars thrown to St. Joseph's feet guarding the place. I walk around number twenty-six to warm down, then take a slow jog along the sunny crest of a wide hill. Some imp lays me down to do ten pushups on the crest of the hill, ten pushups on the frozen breast of mother earth, at the mother house.

"Kiss the place where late you'll lie." I do. Then jump up with imps. Twenty-five good turns has made me whole body and soul, for twelve minutes, at least. This is my precious best, thrown for a gold coin into the rest of this day.

January 6. Running around in circles is a centering prayer for the body that leaks into the spirit.

As the body sweats and the limbs loosen, the concentric circles of the track grow smaller and smaller, until they converge in a still point. Like the bottom of Dante's icy cone. Except this convergence is heaven.

All distractions and feelings get lost somewhere, dropped off like heavy baggage in the upper circles. At the still point there is only peace, and the presence of God pulling every loose joint and sweating molecule to himself.

January 10. Confectioner's sugar fell in the night, sweetening the roofs and the people beneath.

January 13.

love lit every room
there was no sleep
no snow white angel
my soul to keep
snow white

when the sun
came up a rose
and hung
on a thin rim
I took a shade
to each room

one by one
I closed each
night sun

January 19. At the last bend around Emerson Avenue I meet a dirty, overfed dog with obscene jowls, guarding a dirty yard. Old Cerberus at the gate. The yard looks like hell.

I stop and walk by, asking myself all the while, "Why? The dog is heavily chained to a stake and will only bark if you run by."

Not so. I've learned. If you get wild enough, you can snap any restraint.

January 21. I wouldn't miss running in a snowstorm for anything. Visibility is fifty feet ahead. All car lights are on. No way of knowing what the feet run over, what lies hidden under six inches of snow powder. Somehow I get caught in the middle of what I take to be the road, between a funeral procession going blindly up the hill and a snowplow coming down. I take my chances with the snowplow.

I run over snow flat-footed like Franco Harris running in the Super Bowl. Just the thought and my feet are air bound. One look down and I see I am snow bound, snow white this day, one caked snow nun loving you, Jesus, underneath.

January 22. In a swirling snowstorm, Ed Ryan is filling up the hearse at Mobil. He shouts, "You can go faster than that, Sister."

"I'll be in your parlor by noon, if I do."

Two gargoyles huddle in the doorway of the Key Bank. They look retarded, but one of them has my number. "She's getting herself in shape."

January 25. "Pre-menopausal women have almost complete protection from coronary artery disease. For this reason, we seldom hear of any women having difficulty with heart problems while running" (Dr. George Sheehan, in *Runner's World,* January 1980).

There are heart problems and there are heart problems.

January 27. I say the Jesus Prayer for Father Norcott, gone to the hospital in an ambulance yesterday.

On Emerson Avenue it occurs to me that I have not been praying for the car people. I think of them as adversaries, mostly, out to skin and splash me. Today I pray for gentleness on both sides.

January 30. Janet's back aches from bending over backward for kindergarten children. With mounds of Icy Hot in each palm, I run up and down her back, up and down on warm grease, rubbing Jesus into the joints and cracks of her back.

February 2. Bev Murphy's shades are down. She sleeps late, heavy with child.

It is the visitation. And aren't we all like Mary, looking for Elizabeth?

I keep thinking—what if there were no angel for the woman, no angel with heavenly wings, that is. What if the only angel was the one within her, telling her softly, but with a certain persistence, that surely she did grow big with Jesus Christ.

And what if the voice grew sometimes softer, and another voice superseded to say she surely did grow big, but with her own self seeking. Some angel of night and dark dreams did this.

And what if she went running to Elizabeth with mixed emotions. Her transformation was obvious; only its source was obscure. And always the confusing voices. Hoping against hope one day. Determined to say nothing the next.

And what if there were no angel for great Elizabeth either. What if the only angel was that mysterious Spirit of God rushing through her, lifting love for joy in her woman's room and sending her running, wrapping arms around, racing the words blessed, so blessed are you filled with God.

Well then, and only then, she will sing in her clear woman's voice. My soul is overwhelmed in God my savior. In you, my Elizabeth.

And aren't we all looking for Elizabeth?

February 6. A kind of love letter.

Soft dust of snow makes this a quiet morning, a soft, grey day to slow down my life.

There are signs of love in Murphy's window—four paper cut-out hearts the boys put there. There are signs of death at Ryan's—grey flags atop the funeral cars.

The black hearse makes a right off Genesee Street and lifts slowly up and past me into the parking lot. Black cat across your path, some might say. I touch a red mitten gently to the back door of the hearse. Over to the side of the parking lot, Ed is reading a list—who will ride with whom. One we know will ride alone, brother or sister of mine in a black box car.

May the Lord Jesus grab you in his Atlas arms, box and all, and carry you home, his buried treasure found in a field.

One block down, I wave a red mitten to Jack, sitting in his car at the Mobil pump. Four blocks later he catches me leaping over a row of trash cans, outside Jocko's Shebeen.

"Too cold for acrobatics, Sister."

"I just had to try it."

"What? Lifting yourself up by your shoestrings?"

"No. Grabbing hold of the Atlas arms of Jesus, Jack."

The sign outside Jocko's Shebeen came down in the storm. There are signs up and down the whole route, but my favorite runs across the side of the truck parked outside Lipe-Rollway. HEAVY DUTY CLUTCHES. Everytime I see that sign, I think of you.

February 12. All things frosted hold their frozen poses.

February 14. It's a morning for dogs and bandits. Everybody's dog is let out early, to get first crack at the garbage before the trucks come. I outrun one dog and outfox another. While he sniffs, I sprint by and out of sight.

The only parts of me that show are my eyes, bleary in the cold. I pull a white hat down to my eyebrows and a red

33

and white scarf up to my eyelids. I wear the scarf around my mouth and nose like a bandit, like a thief up to my eyeballs. The masked bandit jogs again, through the cold and broken streets of the parish, saying the Jesus Prayer, stealing the people, unaware.

year two

Somewhere in the middle of the running, I started a diary. Mostly because of the lumps. It happened this way.

Once upon a time, in the house of Joe and Connie Wojdyla, there was a window. It was very tall and very wide, the pride of the upstairs flat. Across the top, the window had a beautiful stained glass border, as if its head were still in heaven. The rest of the window, three quarters of it in fact, was clear glass, giving an unobstructed view of the world outside.

For once, it seemed, heaven and earth were united in a single view. In the window.

Once upon the same time, there was a Sister who liked to stretch in the window. She liked to stretch before the row of houses, up on the hill across the street. She liked it best in winter, when the camouflage of leaves was down and she and the houses could face one another, eye to eye. Except most of the houses lowered their shades in winter.

Early mornings in winter, the houses across the street lifted their blind faces up into the rising sun. She stretched in the window then, with her back to the sun, watching it light up the fronts of the houses. She watched the sun rise indirectly, as reflected in other people's faces. She liked second hand.

On the porch outside the window with the heavenly head, there lay a discarded Christmas tree. This story I am telling you took place around that tree.

Open the window then, and bring the tree back inside the small apartment. Stand it in the center of the room with the red rug and put the homemade ornaments back on the branches. Surround the tree with all the loving and waiting of Christmas. It is early Saturday morning, two days before the birth of Christ.

One Sister is running bath water. The other is stretched out flat, cooling down in front of the Christmas tree. She jogs, not unusually well or long, but she does run daily. She also prays faithfully, eats right, lives right, tries to do right, but for the last three days she has noticed a small irritation when she runs. She thinks it is her thermal underwear. She thinks it may be all the Christmas cleaning. A pulled muscle. A strained shoulder. An old second hand bra. A gathering irritation in her left breast.

She feels for lumps, there in front of the tree, and finds only irritation. And ribs. She feels her right side for comparison, to assure herself that she's made the same on both sides, well-balanced, and she puts her hand directly on a marble.

"It's a lump," she cries to her friend taking a bath on the other side of the door. "It's like a marble. I can pick it up in my fingers."

She feels stupor and terror together.

She feels she should have looked more lovingly at spring last year because there won't be another.

She feels at the edge, and all the days she thought were hers are fallen off the edge, into darkness.

She feels the Christmas tree ornaments are exceedingly thin and her friend headed for months of bedpans and sorrow.

She feels cut and stitched flat, shrunk forward because the stitching is too tight and she screams to stand up straight and split open.

She feels the window of heaven and earth is a mockery.

She knows she should open her hands to receive the will of God. She feels the stick crack down on her open hands, the unseen assailant cracking the innocent palms of the second grade child.

She sees the new stick pin in her friend's collar. It says JESUS IS LORD. She wishes Jesus would brand the words across her forehead, because she feels nothing. But she holds onto the words and she holds onto the friend wearing them, holds on for dear life.

"It's a lump all right, Sister, one in each breast. I'll try to reach your regular doctor and make an appointment for the day after Christmas. He'll do a biopsy. Take a sample, freeze it, test it, and, if it's malignant, do a mastectomy. I'll have him call you when you get home."

So slowly they leave the doctor's office, hand in hand and heavy of heart, trying to absorb the consequences of one blow before they reach home to take another. The doctor's office is situated in a far off country, or so it seems. The doctor himself is a foreigner. She feels that anything that happens on Saturday has no relationship whatsoever to the rest of the normal week. She feels she is carrying a very large steely for a heart.

This story ends twenty-four hours later, in a hospital emergency room, where her doctor drains the fluid off into a needle. Or tries to. On impact, the needle shatters all over her chest. Her eyes never leave the doctor's face. Apologetic, he tries again and in thirty seconds deflates two lumps. Her friend rushes to the table and kisses the doctor's hands.

Now and then a lump returns. Now and then she wonders if God will exact a pound of flesh nearest the heart. Sometimes the two friends sit together in the window of heaven and earth and talk about these things.

Soon after, she started to keep a diary, as if each day were a special event, not to be missed.

February 29. One day to spare this year, for leapers. It's a cold plus one, so I take an extra warmup, Rossini's "Overture to a Sleeping Magpie." Today is his birthday. His "Overture" puts the hips into a swivel, arms and legs go metronome.

Still, every part of me freezes once I hit the outside. I pray to Elvis and swivel the last half mile home.

March 2. Sunday silence. Now and then snow squalls. The tall fir tree outside Lipe-Rollway heaves and sighs. There are sea sounds in the fir tree. Squalling in the sky. Groaning deep under the earth where some subterranean beast tosses and turns fitfully, will wake one of these days, give one last heave and roll away winter.

But for today, the wind is king. Sheets of old news flip-flop in the streets, catch around my legs like gaiters.

March 7. It is a very strange thing how a sound has the power to evoke a full-blown picture.

As soon as Luciano Pavarotti begins the aria from La Bohème, I begin stretching, but not on the floor in this apartment. With one note, I am five years old, in another second floor apartment on the other side of town, where on Sunday noon in a steamy kitchen spaghetti water boils in a mélange of kettles, and the lids pop to the melodic rolls of some baritone or other pleading the cause of love in those rich exaggerated tones that quite captivate the pots and lids and little girl's heart. The Italian hour was as integral to the Sunday liturgy as the spaghetti.

Music was all my father's doing—opera on the radio and piano lessons for his first born, though where he found fifty cents a week for the kindly old music teacher I do not know, he in those workman's sleeveless undershirts he still wears.

You can never say thank you. You can only repay in kind somewhere else.

March 8.

Dear Marie,

Today before jogging, I prayed my way through the story of the prodigal son, as I have done many times before. Only today my head kept slipping off on side routes, and I heard the story in a bad translation.

"B" had everything in life—talent, home, security, and most of all, loving friend "A." One day "B" said, "I'm

40

going off to a distant place with what is mine." And "A" was very sad.

On and on my head went, off on a jog for who knows how long in the wrong direction.

Soon "B" returned. "A" said, "I'm glad you've come to your senses, but you see, in the meantime, "C" and I have been managing nicely. It's a hard lesson you have to learn, I know."

Finally, the real story swung back into focus and stopped, at the rich garments coming down and rings for the fingers. The story refused to budge, would not go on to the end, though I knew the rest of it.

Calling it quits, I put on my jogging shoes, looked at the clock, and realized that you were saying goodbye to your brother Jimmy, in Callahan's funeral parlor, one hundred and fifty miles away. Somewhere in the lacing of my shoes, I saw the rich robes come down over Jimmy's head, and rings on his hands.

Then I knew why the story had stopped. There was no more.

Your brother is home.

March 9.

snow scene

the blanket is not
on the ground
as in "blanketed with snow"
but lies upright
in the sky
a veritable snow screen
against the eye
and for it too.
the barrel is not
upright but fallen

41

flat on its face
on the ground
flat on its side
under the blanket
of snow screen
impossible to hide.
the woman is not
on the ground
but under it
in a barrel
riding the fall
of veritable snow
screening always
as in "always love you."

March 10.

One foot is Mary, wanting to stay put.
The other foot is Martha, itching to go.

March 11. Everybody out here knows that winter has done its worst and, considering the area of the country, there really wasn't much winter to speak of. So we don't. We give knowing looks and keep the word snug under our knit hats.

Heaven is in a howl and earth in a minus twenty wind chill. But we're still footing it, in the face of the high rising gas price. Every leg has a price tag on it now. Let's hear it for the fifty cent run to the drugstore, the one dollar jog downtown and back.

The wind takes my breath away and leaves me with a ten cent whistle in my chest.

March 12.

What's blue and white and blinding all over?
The winter of unknowing.
How do you run in such a winter?
Over the slick spine of Jesus, into the forty mile an
   hour cloud.
Whom do you meet in the cloud?
Our former landlady, who evicted us.
What do you say?
Hi.

March 19.

March 19. Winter went this St. Joseph's day. Overhead the screeching geese return, flying an unsure curve.

March 21.

March 21. Every day before I run, I sit as prayerfully as I can and read one of your Jesus stories, for an hour or so. For twenty-one years, I have been turning these pages faithfully, listening to your Voice spin a tale through my heart and guts and life.

Once upon a time
    there was a farmer who went out sowing, and . . .
    another farmer who sowed good seed in his field,
      but . . .
    a woman who lost a small coin somewhere in the
      house, and . . .
    a rich man who dressed in purple and linen and . . .
    a woman with a package of yeast who . . .
    a certain eminent judge in a certain city who . . .

Then there are the stories other people tell about you.
One day the mother of Zebedee's sons came up to him and . . .
    some Sadducees came up to him and . . .
    a leper came up to him and . . .

a woman with a jar of heavy perfume came up to
   him and . . .
two blind men (believe it or not) came up to him
   out on the road
and followed him all the way home where they
   cornered him and . . .
a man with an unclean spirit came up to him and . . .
his mother and brothers came and had to wait
   outside for him to come up to them. And . . .

One day you were walking along the sea,
   walking through a wheat field,
   walking into the temple,
         and out again,
   walking past Levi's tax table,
   walking into Capernaum,
   walking into Peter's house where you hoped to sit
   down to dinner.

Then one day you walked into a place called Gethse-
mani and never walked out. Soon stories that seemed like
nonsense started,
      about your walking up behind Mary Magdalene in
         the garden and . . .
      about your walking up behind two friends on the
         Emmaus road and . . .
      about your walking through closed doors and hearts.

And now I would like to tell *you* a story about what I've
got hidden in this convoluted heart of mine.

April 3. Holy Thursday. They're carrying in the new boards
at Kerstetter's, for Crossroads Kitchens.

April 4. Good Friday.

Poeta

I am an old woman, respect my lines,
shaking out a brown bag in the wind.
All my words are gone, the songs are dead.
No laurel leaf on my head.
But the hearth is warm
and I shall lie down in ease.
Catch as catch can on a summer breeze.
Old women dream in minor keys.

April 6. Easter. Early in the morning, on the first day of the
week, I am out running in the Easter sun. The cars move
bumper to bumper through Cookie Caloia's dark wash,
come out born again. I know he is not in the dark tomb. I
know he walks the parish streets with the wounds of his vic-
tory, as they say, showing. Still, I am surprised to meet the
ones who died this Lent also out in the Easter sun.

Jimmy Bonville wears his heart on his sleeve like a stop-
watch stopped. Cousin Richard walks into heaven for his
thirty-seventh year with the marks of the measles still on his
face. Fairest of all is Aunt Anne, luminescent in the long
white lace and silk dress she wore for her daughter's wedding ten years ago. She wears it today for the Bridegroom
with the holes in his hands and feet. At the hem of her gown,
Aunt Anne's ankles are swollen with water.

Chrissy Susnock stumbles up the hill in first heels, her
broken arms healed, well concealed in the sleeves of the
boxy new Easter coat. You're in the wrong procession,
Chrissy. So am I.

Not so. There are no lines drawn in the company of
saints.

April 20.

> Sweet choral song of birds in the tree.
> One prophetic voice in another key.
> Squawk among squeaks.

April 23. There's a strange feeling in the house, as if some-body walked in while I was out running. I leave the door un-locked—there's nothing to steal. Except the Sacrament. I'm not sure he can take care of himself.

April 26. First I meet the barking dog. One block later—the barking man.

"You have to go faster than that, Lady."

"You're going downhill."

"I walk seven to eight miles a day, Dolly."

At Mobil I catch sight of Jack Chase with the shades on, his gold afro in the sun like a halo, like a Botticelli angel. He smiles. I wave. You redeem the day, Jack.

April 27. Ten feet ahead there's a car parked outside Jocko's Shebeen. A man sits in the front seat, with a woman's head laid back and cradled in the crook of his arm. Her eyes are closed. She looks sick.

As I pass the car, I see it's only spring fever, only love in the lap of the man in the front seat of the car.

She turns in the cradle to look out the window at me looking in. We're sweating on both sides of the window this cool, gold morning.

April 30.

Dear Joyce,

I have been intending to write you this letter for weeks. Maybe even years. Today, I have no choice.

In the back seat of our car we carry an empty grey frame. It's called "Emmaus."

What is an Emmaus frame? It's when you pray and pray your heart out, round and round the four corners of the Scriptures, hearing God's voice burn a way through your convoluted heart. Then suddenly, there's no voice. And in some silent, ridiculous act of breaking, you see him. But he's gone before you can say it. Still, the pinpoint of light in the frame of the heart lasts a lifetime.

Or again, an Emmaus frame is when two people talk and talk round and round the four sides of the matter with their hearts burning up inside them and suddenly stop, and look at one another. Maybe for the first time. Maybe for the only time. No matter. The look lasts a lifetime in the frame of the heart.

You and I made an Emmaus frame years ago, the night we talked and talked our way across town to Karen's Donuts, into the shop and out and back into your father's red car, on either side of the stick shift you loved so well, with the donut bag opened between us. Then, for no reason, we took a long look into each other. And I saw you for the first time. It has lasted a lifetime in the frame of my heart.

It's ridiculous to add this, but we had just broken a donut.

Every day I jog around an Emmaus frame. I'm making it larger and larger these days. This morning I ran a four mile frame, through the parish, praying the name of Jesus that the Altar Rosary Society would help support my work. I had one block to finish on the Jesus frame when Barbara Jakubowski rolled up, pulled over, swung open the door and exclaimed yes, they were going to give me a large donation. We shouted and cried, blessed God and each other. Then she handed me a bag. In it were two donuts.

So I send you an empty Emmaus frame, Joyce. We come to know him in the breaking of donuts.

May 1. A dull and uniformly grey world with a soft shoulder, as a shoulder should.

May 4. Jubilee celebration at the mother house. Eleanor Ceccucci leads the procession with the Cross of Christ held high, the eye of God stitched large in front.

Hold high the Cross, Eleanor, high, high, straight and true.

She does not hear, holds the Cross, as a matter of fact, on a definite slant, through the narrow gate.

May 5. For a novice.

Yesterday morning, as you know, I ran twenty-five circles around St. Joseph, for Marie Bonville's silver jubilee. But I was chased by Worry, who had done the New York State Thruway in record time to find me and dog me down the mother house front.

When Worry tired, he passed the baton to Boredom, and I thought the run around those circles would never end.

Back home today I do three miles easily, up and down the rough terrain, and conclude that running around bored in a narrow, confined structure has made it easy to run farther and longer on normal streets.

I hope it may be so for you.

May 8.

Wise spiders catch pearls
early in the morning,
spread a fine network
of lights under a bush.
They spin their hearts out
stringing pearls of great price.

May 11. Run early, while my mother sleeps, to slip the oversized Mother's Day card between her doors.

Later comes the steady stream of children and grandchildren, into every nook and cranny of the place, through the
turkey dinner and into the late day sandwiches stuffed with
the remains. The grandchildren coo on beds, crawl, stagger,
and leap the floors, down under the smokey cigar curls. The
mother is content in their midst, content too when they leave
and she can settle into the Sunday paper. At least it seems so,
until she says of the one who did not come, "He didn't even
call. Did you know that?"

All day long her eyes had left the ninety-nine nearest
her to search for the missing one.

May 13. Running in a rainy world, up greasy Milton Avenue to the post office, I sidestep a rotund woman encased in
yellow isinglass, a steaming greenhouse. Her face blossoms,
booms, "Do you run in the rain?"

"Sure. Why not?"

Why not, indeed, over the slick slime, under the sleazy
sign for exotic dancers alias strip teasers, running to keep
body and soul together, yours, theirs, and mine?

May 15. Ascension Thursday. How can I ascend with leaden
feet?

May 16. The smell of lilacs overwhelms the bus exhaust, leaves me running dizzy and backward across city lines into Solvay and up Summit Avenue where piano sounds drift out of the first house at the top left. The home of Mrs. Laura Susco. Or is it Mrs. Flora? Just below the house the lilac blooms in heat.

Inside, Mrs. Susco arranges herself just so on her end of the piano bench, fixes the folds of her dress so the young girl next to her does not see she is pregnant. One wonders if, seeing, she would understand.

God bless you, Mrs. Susco, wherever you are.

May 19. May has known too much of rain and a grey impenetrable heaven. A thick cloud of unknowing. Oh, for a life aligned to your will. Which will I do not know.

Running under the cloud, I keep my eyes fixed on the sidewalk, but it is no comfort. I see there all those unknowing people in the Gospels.

The headwaiter at Cana—he did not know where the choice wine came from.

John the Baptizer—he spent his whole life preparing for the Savior, then didn't know him when he saw him.

The woman at the well did not know who was asking her for a drink.

The two friends on the way to Emmaus didn't know the third man on the road.

Oh, to be sure, there were some who thought they knew. There were the townspeople who said, "Isn't this Jesus, the son of Joseph? We know his father and mother." And thinking they knew, they said of course he couldn't have come from heaven.

And then there is Mary Magdalene, running around the cemetery garden. She seems closest of all. The Lord has been taken away. I do not know where they have put him.

May 20. The fog came down during the night and covers the earth still.

> O God, if you would own me
> find me
> lost somewhere in the fog
> and lonely
> running in a cloud
> not of elements only

May 22. Given short notice that I must move from my workroom in the rectory attic, I run frantic up and down the streets of the parish looking for another place. I note every "for rent" sign along the way. I dream about the "for sale" ones.

My feet take me north to visit a small band of Sisters into yoga, into a lovely house redone in natural boards, into vast fields and hills dotted with small hermitages. Theirs is a spiritual life center where people come to breathe the fresh spiritual air, to enjoy the river, tennis courts and chapel, to work in the gardens. Every room is insulated, winterized, eternalized.

Back home, Janet and I walk the broken streets of the parish, checking all the "for rent" signs.

Mrs. L. fidgets at the idea of renting two rooms in her large, empty upstairs flat. Still, she would like the money. That would be $100, plus heat, lights and water. But no, she had better not. Company comes once a year from Rochester.

Further on up the jogging route, Mr. D. and his small wife show us their abandoned store, show us, rather, the blue sky and green trees through the broken walls and falling ceiling of their store. "We can only rent one half of this. It's only a guess, but it'll cost you $150 a month for heat and lights. We'll have to think about the rent, after we calculate the cost of patching the floor, walls and ceiling. We work hard, my wife and I, but it has to be worth our while."

Next stop is Walker real estate, above the drugstore. Mr. Walker shows us three small rooms for $200 a month.

There are five convents within jogging distance, so we stop at one. We are shown the cellar. "Here is the garbage room. We could put the garbage cans in the garage with the car. But that wouldn't be good."

"Here is the pipe and meter room. The pipes back up now and then, so there will be a little water on the floor."

"Here is a closet. We could give you half."

"Here is a nice room. Some of us type here sometimes. We could give you half."

"Half a closet, half another room. Would that do for your work? We like to keep the guest rooms empty."

So, what's the lesson of the feet, I keep asking, as I jog the broken streets, still looking for a place.

The lesson is you're never going to have a spiritual life center except the one God makes inside that skinny body of yours. But your heart is so cluttered, there's no room. Give him space.

And what's the lesson of the jogging?

How could you forget it, after all this running? Turn back to what you yourself wrote on March 10.

One foot is Mary, wanting to stay put.
The other foot is Martha, itching to go.

The lesson of the jogging is to run on two feet, slowly, carrying the spiritual life center through the parish.

Run slowly. Some days you race. Slow down, so people can get to the center. But keep moving—nobody is staying overnight. There is no river, tennis court, or chapel. Nor will there be.

So stop looking at the "for rent" signs strung out along

your jogging route. Remember what you read this morning out of Janet's book, "Provide for your future by making it more insecure." Martha finds that exciting. Mary knows it is painful. For better or worse, you're an MC—a moving contemplative.

May 24. On the vigil of Pentecost, I run to the rectory attic and find my photographic darkroom dismantled. Someone has put up filigree curtains for the coming of the Holy Spirit. Light streams through every dark place except the heart.

May 25. Today I run in a strong driving wind. How beautiful on the street are the feet of one who brings good news, announcing peace, saying to the people your God loves you. How beautiful on the street. He has only your two feet.

May 30. Hi. Can you tell me the way to Genesee?
    Straight ahead, three or four blocks.
    Good morning. How do I get to Cayuga Street? Where are Cogswell, Olive, Milton, Lewis, Herkimer, General Burgoyne and the whole marching army? Lady, I can't even say it. Where is Coykendall? Where is heaven from here?
    I don't know. I'm just running downtown in my lightweight gown.

June 1. Trinity Sunday. 93% humidity.
    You do batter my heart, three person'd God. Then you steam press a Jesus shirt to my skin. You are a jealous God, relentless.

June 3. Taking my chances in a light rain.
    Two blocks out, of course it pours. Never a sheltering

Today I learn a lesson from the wind:
    It is not always possible to go forward.
    It is always possible to go up and down.

tree when you need one. I run faster in rain—this nag's a mudder. My hair is like soaked clumps of kelp, hanging around the shore of my face where ears run, eyes run, nose runs most of all.

This run's good luck to you, Genuine Risk.

June 5. There is ample evidence that the menstrual cycle has no bearing on a female runner's performance. In the Tokyo Olympics gold medals were won by women in all phases of the menstrual cycle.

Furthermore, a woman's internal and external organs are all adequately supported, so that she can run without jarring anything loose. Use of the bra is completely optional.

June 10. At the corner a red cardinal breakneck speeds out of the Conte bushes, shoots by at the level of the knees and leaves me shaking. Then laughing. All the people at the bus stop laugh.

For the rest of the way the streets are quiet. Frostbitten. The roses have a hangdog look.

Because my eyes are down, I see the crutches first, then the man's empty trouser leg. A small boy in a bright red jacket leads at the level of a cardinal. His eyes are anxious.

June 17. Stella Maris. Nothing is changed here, not in a whole year's passing. The only colors are still vast green and wide, stretchy blue. The firs still throw the same dark morning fingers across the same rolling green. The same rose is about to bloom on the same bush. On the lake the same mother duck swims in the same flotilla of twelve puff balls. The mind labors to insist she was the puff ball last summer, but the thought is thin. The fat lady is still Jesus Christ.

And running the circle out front is nothing new either. My feet follow the same orbit, swing wide on the curves and into post position. Same dogs, same Mary, same feet on the way to the same Elizabeth. Only one thing is changed. It makes all the difference. The fat lady died.

June 18. Nothing fancy, just round and round on a Jesus Prayer with a sinus headache.

June 19. Twenty-five times around the Stella Maris track gets dull, so I divide the run into groups of five, like a rosary.

The first mystery is for novice legs learning all over again each morning how to loosen up, lift and stretch around the track. This run of five is slow and deliberate. Initiation.

The second mystery is for strengthening what the legs learned in the first mystery. For ease and added speed. Confidence.

The third mystery is swift, joyful running. Fun.

My favorite is the fourth. I put my body on cruise and it runs its own course, thoughtlessly, evenly. I never knew I came with cruise.

The last mystery is coming home. I run a lap of confidence, fun, cruise, a few fast sprints, and a slow walk around, looking for the cardinal who has been laughing at all these shenanigans.

June 20. After the circle, I make a straight line down toward the town and wherever the run takes me.

I'm hot off the hill when I see him, leaping and twisting in high air outside St. James Episcopal Church, young man in the red roller skates. His long legs are like scissors on a loose bolt, cutting X's all over the sidewalk of St. James. When he isn't leaping for high joy, that is.

It's those loose X's I love and he sees it, decides to roll with my run, and swings an arm around my shoulder. I grab his shirt and off we go through town—red roller man, woman in the star spangled feet. I run straight forward. He rolls forward by swinging sideward.

It's soon all too clear that my straight line does not coincide with his X. Just a matter of style. We put a little space between us, then run and roll a sweet pace up Fennel Street and back.

June 23. Back home, nun on a hot sidewalk blesses you, old man with the cane and the stunned left side.

June 28. Today, only a few miles away, a fifty-seven year old jogger collapsed and died, during the Grace Assembly of God's annual "Run for the Son."

According to the Rev. Glass, church pastor, his parishioner believed in God and physical fitness. He was faithful to the church's Thursday morning prayer meetings. First he would run three miles and then come in and pray.

Today he hung up his shoes, an offering to God.

June 29. Late afternoon, under a white, impervious heaven. I'm out for a second run, trying to put my insides in order.

After jogging, I walk around to the backyard and lose myself in a bank of orange tiger lilies. I keep an eye out for escape hatches—those openings between the houses, or those dark green holes the trees make in their overlapping.

Soon, darkness comes up from under the tiger lilies. In the middle of the dark orange bank, twenty-five lavish bunches of Easter lilies sway on impossible heights, their white heads luminous and ghostly. No trumpets sound. Not a murmur in the knitting of night.

Not a murmur until Agnes next door screams from one of the dark green holes, screams at her other neighbor and his wild dog. Something about Sunday being a day of rest.

She slams her way indoors and, laying her strong gardener's hands on the piano, she strangles bunches of white keys. As Time Goes By. She pounds the board in one key and sings in another. She works her way to a climactic death rattle, a torturous glide up and down the guts of the piano, the shattering of nerves.

Then the trees start. And the rains. And the tornado warning is in effect. Lines go down, lights go out. In the window of heaven and earth I worry for the trees, worry for the cars and the people in them, worry for all the inhabitants of dark holes, worry in the dark twisted passages of my own heart made manifest this day.

June 30. The labyrinth was built by Daedalus, a most skillful artificer. It was an edifice with numberless winding passages and turnings opening into one another, and seeming to have neither beginning nor end. The labyrinth was so artfully contrived, that whoever was enclosed in it could by no means find a way out unassisted.

In the twisted passages of the labyrinth there roamed a minotaur, a monster who was half animal, half human. The minotaur was exceedingly strong and fierce (Thomas Bulfinch, *Bulfinch's Mythology,* Thomas Y. Crowell Company, New York, 1947, pp. 152, 156).

One day the maker of winding passages found herself shut up in the dark corridors of her own making, facing the monster exceedingly strong and fierce.

"Who will give me a sharp edged sword to slay this beast? And where shall I find a ball of string, that I may unravel it and find my way back out of these twisted channels?"

This diary is your ball of thread. You can trace your way back whenever you will.

"And the sword?"

Put on your Jesus shoes and run a middle course through the labyrinth.

The Stella Maris Retreat House

"Look at my Jesus shoes. They're broken, and the toes have come through in holes the size of quarters."

It doesn't matter. Tie the laces a little tighter. You will run on snakes and scorpions, but nothing shall ever harm you. Your name is written in heaven.

"And what about my labyrinthine heart?"

Stay near him and you will be safe.

July 1. Suddenly I catch myself racing in the heat, with stride like wide calipers, and the easy roll of sockets and joints. It's the thought of Indians that catches me, the thought of Tekakwitha beatified, Tekakwitha Indian running in soft feet and swift up Harbor Street and across the overgrown Lipe-Rollway field where she stops, just barely, to swoop up great handfuls of white white daisies, every one a sun center she runs with.

July 3.

> neighbor . . . From the belt down she bulges badly,
> double-barrels out the back door
> towards work as if fueled and fired.
> There was a fire here once
> as burnt out butts of grass attest.
> A two-sided rust-backed bug
> with green head and patterned belly
> shoves its weight around grass
> laid in passive attitudes.
> Ply your cumbersome trade,
> bug dragging bulging gear,
> then break open your rust back
> and fly out of here.

July 7. Stella Maris. Her face is sallow and bloated, her arms locked across her front like a chastity belt. Her hands are all wrapped up in her rosary, but she has seen me before I notice her.

Still she cannot bring herself to acknowledge my presence. Once she could not bring herself to approve my taking religious vows.

How our sins do circle to haunt us.

All the women of the Altar Rosary Society return too. How could I forget, you who keep me running the prayer circle? I see you each one. Agnes Gibbons running the iron up and down the altar cloth. Mrs. Judge whose ironing days are over. Ann Cedrone hanging out a wet harvest on lines the top of the hill, catching wind of Genevieve Federico on the church organ. Mary Vanelli walking the dog, walking her mind, walking her children's children. Delores Bottrill threading her way to work through the eye of the 690 needle. Connie Wojdyla lifting heavy feet at the IGA. Janet Sheehan lifting heavy feet at Tops. Angie Morrison cleaning chicken for the priests' supper and worrying about her cancer. Mrs. DeFabio worrying about her dead son. Florence Monnat worrying not at all about managing affairs on the first floor of the rectory.

Two hundred and fifty-nine women, each lighting a thick waxen candle, and I with head afire and waxen feet. The whole altar is banked in red vigil.

And seeing the crowd, his heart is moved to pity.

And all, all of these things are saved in the heart of Jesus, who carries our burdens and brightens.

July 8. Five miles yesterday. Back to three today.

> Tired of looking at things eternal,
> I put my ear to the rind of a tree
> and listen to the wind in the hollow.

July 9. On the lake a power boat and skier cut a white slit up the non-resisting sea. On shore, we watch with different eyes now. Last week, four miles down, a boatman looked back at his fallen skier and cut two little girls to death. You can't have eyes front and back.

My sport is non-competitive, non-violent running. Runners do not cut, kick, tackle, cripple, or punch anyone. On the contrary, runners take any blows to be given. I have been hit by car, bike, and verbal abuse. Always from behind.

July 13. After jogging, I follow my nose into the kitchen. Aimée, meaning love, makes the bread they sell to build the chapel. The way she works the dough you know she is the bread.

July 14. This morning I do my stretch exercises on a tree out front and find ants streaming out of a knothole.

> Daredevil ants
> ride
> the spine
> of a tree
> for a freeway
> collide
> rather than
> yield
> know no
> caution
> like the old
> lady
> in the red
> hardtop
> black dots
> atop
> and white headlights

crawling
a single lane
stalk
and falling
thereby proving
all laws
relative
to break-
neck
speeds
relative.

July 15. I love the heft of you, Jesus icon on my back. A
man could run shirtless for all to see. A woman lets you in to
sing in a rib cage caged with those ah! bright wings of yours.
For all the world to hear.

July 18. My run takes me through the busy town and up the
hill to the cemetery. It's a good workout, the rolling hills in
the cemetery, and very interesting. I run slowly, so I can
read the stones.

The men have names like Philo, Franklin, Porter, Julius,
Augustus, and lots of Samuels. There lie Joshua, Elijah,
Ajah, Asa, Ezra, Isaac, Daniel and Job. Followed by Simeon,
Ebenezer, Nathaniel, Mortimer, Horace, Winslow and Jona-
than Edwards, after the Puritan preacher who called us sin-
ners in the hands of an angry God.

There is more variety among the women. There are, of
course, Old Testament names like Rebecca, Esther, and
Sarah, a favorite. Then come the virtues, of sorts—Temper-
ance, Grace and Desire. After that it's free reign with So-
phia, Samantha, Sabrina, Mabel, Isabel, Abigail and Medora.
My favorites are Lettie, Lottie, Addie, Fannie, Minnie, Bessie, whose stone is there without her, and Amie May. Hers
has a cryptic four line message, half erased. Did her parents,

Charles and Martha, know any more about death than we do, the day they buried her? Or did they simply take the lines from a funeral director's catalogue? Even so, it would be good to read the words.

Relationships, on the other hand, are clear to see—wife, husband, daughter, children, a large marker for a whole clan of brothers, their wives and children. Fred lies with a wife on either side. Salmon and Jerusha lie together.

Some stones boast of years—"79 yrs. 2 m. & 13 ds." Others proclaim relationships—"my husband," "baby," "only son," "our mother," "formerly of England." A few promise "perpetual care" and "endowment." There is a nameless daughter who died the day she was born, and a mystery stone marked "L. S. F. L."

Frederick and Editha Webber lie with the three little children they buried in 1884—Charlie, Jeannette and Edith. Was there a fire? An epidemic? Did the distraught parents have any more children? Maybe. There is a stone nearby for Lottie, born five years after the tragedy.

Down near the entrance of the cemetery, five laughing men are digging a new grave.

Two blocks away at the lake, a young man struts the boardwalk. He swings his water skis heavenward.

July 22. Our Lady of Calvary. Farmington, Connecticut.

I am here making a retreat, with a bee sting and a bloated left hand. My arm is in a sling, but I'm out to run anyway, a one armed bandit, about to be taken.

A small flight of stairs leads up to a round grassy tableland, with the fourteen stations of the cross spaced around the rim. At the head is a tableau of Christ crucified and mourners.

The walkway is narrow, broken, strewn with fir tree debris and a patch of green moss. In three places tree roots have risen to make tricky hurdles, not a step apart. The whole circle is tight, only one hundred and fifty steps, with sharp steep curves and quick drops, perhaps a meditative assist to those making a slow way of the cross. I take a challenging forty laps with the crucifixion on my left, and on my right, far off in the town, the needle thin steeple of the Congregationalist church.

Same legs and feet in the same broken shoes run easily and as usual although the place is strange and far from home. The same old blue shirt soaks up sweat and sticks like a second skin, as always.

"This is how close to you I long to be. And am. As always."

July 23. Peaceful. Rain like a gauzy veil over a dark green runner's circle. Inside the house someone's having music for breakfast.

The oratorio she sings is a mystery to me, but something about her dark alto, and those soft brooding baritones, is sustaining, and I know I too have looked on the darkest things and come out live.

July 24. The sun rises in the tree paradoxically, by descending. Lying down, I look up at the rising tree, to its topmost part. And the tree says, "Endure."

Endure. Oh, to be sure there is a price to pay—the leaves are fewer than before (as with a man going bald) and many bare branches, there in the topmost part, but this only makes truer the word of the rising tree. Endure. All love can.

July 26. Feast of Saints Ann and Joachim, grandparents.

My grandparents seemed to me always old. At least that is how I remember them, in their extremities.

Grandpa Sauro, with the eldest son of the next three generations—my father, brother and nephew. My grandfather was an old brown oak leaf. Carefully opened, he told wise and funny stories.

Grandma Sauro was a big woman and, at the end, painfully fat. When the last stay gave way she melted into eternity.

Grandpa Sauro, on the other hand, was a brown oak leaf, shriveled and curled. Carefully opened, he told wise and funny stories.

The day we buried Aunt Margaret, Grandma Rose on my mother's side tried to throw herself into the grave. One month later she did.

Grandpa Gangemi lived the longest. He smoked stogies, drank wine, went blind, and entered heaven that way.

Today, for the first time, I realize that all of my grandparents are gone. Not, however, without leaving me gifts. When it came time to divide Grandpa Sauro's small legacy, his youngest child got the house. His eldest grandchild got the stories.

July 27. On the third lap a canine large leaps onto the circle, for fun, I guess, his long tongue lolling over tooth and fang.

No fun for me, though. Bravely, I say "Sit," and, after a fashion, he does, on the edge of the circle, so that every lap is a slip and slide past Cerberus. On the thirteenth round I quit, wishing people with animals would realize not everyone shares their doggy fondness.

But this is only because I do not like dogs.

July 28. For my spiritual director.

Today you told me to run to the waterfall. Right then I suspected something because I had just finished reading Arturo Vivante's story, "Run to the Waterfall." But you could never have known that.

Then you gave me those strange directions—run down Calvary hill, take a right to the street main, turn right and take the first left all the way on the street straight.

Somehow, I found the place. Your waterfall was not

what I had expected. It powered a mill. And the mill was not what I would have expected either. I know what a watermill should be, nestled in a green wood, with an old wheel of rickety wood that creaks with the slow turning. Well, your watermill was in a green wood, but there the resemblance ended. The lovely mill was a high-power generator. The waterwheel was prone, steel, and indoors. I enjoyed it as best I could.

Then I noticed a bookstore attached to the other side of the mill. Here was the wonderland I had been looking for, and, I admit, I wandered like Alice from niche to stall to barrel to shelf and back again. Longer than befits one making a retreat. Please accept this small book of poetry. Count it as a gift from the waterfall windmill.

Nor was that all. I ran back on the street straight, in record time, stopped for traffic at the intersection with street main, and in the pause noticed a sign there—Maiden Lane. Just then a station wagon rolled up to a stop, and my eyes lowered to discover a fair haired maiden behind the wheel of the car stopped under the sign Maiden Lane. A smile started before I remembered my manners. Too late. The maiden smiled broadly, filling the car with light, and two strangers met in a still point. I shall never see her again, but I shall know her anywhere in heaven.

Your run to the waterfall was other than I had expected. And so much more. All along you have been trying to tell me this.

July 30. There ought really to be a gathering, here on the commons, in Farmington, Connecticut. Let there be a coming together before we go home.

Let there come Cowle and Pitkin, Hooker, Hart and Porter, each bearing the sign posted over his door with his name and date. For the town is filled with signs saying "circa" 1660, 1725, 1749.

The Harts and Porters lie in the town cemetery now.

Their artifacts are gathered in the Farmington Museum.

This is how we lived and came together. This is how we took care of our old. This is how we washed, cooked, ate, slept, cared for our children, worshiped God, and fought, always the worst battles within the walls. The needle thin spire of the First Church of Christ, Congregationalist, is testimony. We did our best. Take what is helpful.

Each of us is a needle thin spire skyward, testifying I am of this place, of this time, of this people, worshiping this God. We do our best. Take what is helpful.

Up the hill from the town, at Our Lady of Calvary Retreat House, the arms of God stretch east and west, gathering together the farthest reaches of the sea past and future. Jesus is himself a thin spire Christ fixed in time, knowing full well he comes from God and is going to God.

We have only this time and this place to seek to know.

August 5. Running enlarges the heart. So does praying.

August 6.

transfiguration

A white paper moth cradles in the crotch
of three young blades of grass that twitches
where it itches with ants;

how the world flinches with the pinches of God.
Spiders shimmy invisible wires
over snap crackle and pop

goes the plot below.
A ghostly moth exhumes the cradle
to spreadeagle a white paper fan.

August 10. Ithaca, New York. Clown ministry workshop.

I have run with hands full—of letters, cards, and packages to mail, a quart of milk, a loaf of bread, the Sunday paper folded flat and the money to buy these things. Library books, up to three in each hand. A bottle of eucharistic wine, three pounds of Yashika camera, a wild bunch of white daisies with sun centers. Except for the daisies, nothing is so light as the balloons I run with now, fifty helium balls with "love" writ large on every one, running through the streets of Ithaca on feet light indeed, the vanguard, troubador of the circus parade. A clown of an Olympic torchbearer.

At the nursing home the men and women are already gathered outside, waiting. A few watch in open windows above. I stop and pass a love balloon to each one, hand to hand resuscitation, until the parade arrives and the Salvation Army Band.

August 18. Birthday. Thank you for new running shoes. They feel like fifty helium balloons rising, love writ large all over.

Thank you for a new Jesus shirt (sticking to me closer than ever) and for short shorts, long legs.

Thank you for the jacket with the Sponsor's name stitched over the heart.

Thank you for the jogometer that ticks on my hip like a misplaced heart. Today I measure the miles to heaven. It's farther than I thought. Come with me.

I love the runner's world you give me. Help me make it wider.

August 23. The young husband in the flat next door uses his feet to kick his wife. She holds their month-old child. I run out on the porch, wishing in some way to stand with her, feeling ineffectual. They leave in a broken down car, broken down marriage.

I look at my two feet.

Then I notice the young husband on the other side of us, heavy, with a girlish face. He has stopped clipping his bushes. He seems gentle enough. I pray for his feet, and his wife inside with the child inside.

August 26.

> Let your words stay part of me,
> become a pear, a peach, sweet grapes
> on the vine, a cup of red wine.

August 27. Run in an upright position with your back straight and erect. No exaggerated lean forward. Run tall, trunk over legs, eyes straight ahead. Remember that plumb line running through your center from legs to head and heavenward, held by the hand of God.

August 28. They call a day like this "clammy"—hot, damp and windy. Take a dry mop to the air and the mop will ring wet.

For some unknown reason, I'm running like a vigilante, sweeping the sidewalks clean. A frightened cat dashes left, a flock of brown birds swoops up and away. Underfoot, a spider hurries on a hundred legs.

At the end of Fayette, where the trucks and campers horde the sidewalk and make a blind curve, four men pick their cautious way into the street, and around their own obstacles. Jet propelled, I take the outside lane, just barely, and think of Jack Tatum on the football field. "They call me assassin." A body in motion, he says, always has the advantage.

They call me sweeper.

September 2. Tribute to Joan of Arc.

Some wild wind is punching the candle flame down with left jabs and fierce right hooks. The flame takes it all on the chin, dances back and forth around the ring and ends up upright, hands above head in a single thread of praise.

Outside, the sky is lightened after a night of rain, having dumped its load of sorrow on the backs of trees. They droop and drag the earth, spread out arms for a slow drying.

I run in the tentative coming of sun.

September 3. Windless, soundless, cloudless and blue. The sun sings on the wires overhead and a wing tail silver bird flies south, taking a piece of the sun with it. Lewis Park is under a spell, the swings in a trance on the ends of chains. Underfoot the grass is matted from summer. A Yankees hardhat hangs retired on the gate. Not a leaf stirs. Nor child. Nor dog. Penny loves Dave forever on the clubhouse wall.

On the edge of the park, the windows at St. Brigid's School are thrown open. Someone is warming up the piano. It is the opening day of school.

It is also the year of the backpack bookbag. I'm running late behind Pinocchio, Mickey Mouse, Bugs Bunny, the 64 Crayola and the American Boy Scout, behind brown backpacks with straps for shoulders and straps for hands, behind yellow ones, green ones, blue ones, and Adam D'Agostino in a red backpack half his height.

73

"What do you carry in those backpacks?"

"Everything." Sure enough—books, bingo chips, lunch money, milk money, Holly Hobby Wishingwell Games, pencils and erasers, patrol slips, belts and badges, bandaids, paint shirts, kleenex and the muppets.

"How about lunch?"

"That goes in these lunch boxes." These lunch boxes look like mini billboards, painted bright with school buses, Disney World, Pigs in Space, Peanuts and Snoopy, the New York Giants, the Roller Skater, the Battle of the Planets and the Empire Strikes Back.

"Turn yourself into a kid, Sister, and get a lunch box."

"I will. What's in yours?"

"Pressed ham. I love pressed ham."

All the dresses are fluffed on the first day of school, with the little brown legs of summer underneath. All the jeans are stiff and new and standing on their own in the schoolyard. For some children it is the first day of school ever.

She is in dark glasses. Her son is in a two-piece blue suit. She is smiling. He won't let go of her hand. Or is it she won't let go?

"Hi. My name is Johnny Halpin. This is my friend, Peanuts."

A diminutive child smiles, her hair swept up in ribbons, showing little pierced ears.

Mom with a loving left arm nudges little saddle shoes with two inch soles and great traction toward the kindergarten door and Sister Janet. Sister Janet already has her hands full of Cindy, hiding behind her mother and holding her hand fiercely. Janet slips her hand between mother and child, making a bridge. Adam in the red backpack says, "It's not so bad after all."

The children all go in. The mothers all go home. From out the windows facing Lewis Park come little bird voices. "Dear God   bless me   as I start   kindergarten."

74

September 7. When the moon is in Virgo we eat less, wear less, feel chilly, run a little farther, take Mercury along with winged feet, make peace, make bread and bring it to the hungry and generally purify our lives.

Today I run not with Mercury, but with Janet. It is our fourth or fifth run together. All I need do is slow down to a conversational pace and we run the same rhythm.

At the corner I spot a discarded Sunday paper and pick it up. Once home, Janet's eye spots the headline, RUNNERS TO SET PACE FOR UNITED WAY.

"We've just run two miles together," she says. "We can build it up to three and four tenths by September 28. Let's."

I avoid races of any kind. But who can discourage such optimism?

September 8. Here the preparations for the race begin. I have it in my mind (and legs) to run as fast as I can, and take off like a flying dervish in the direction of Solvay. Before long I'm cramped and coughing up belch from the Allied Chemical Company. Still, I do not slow down. The run seems endless.

When I reach home, the jogometer says 3.1 miles. The clock says fifteen minutes. And I am astounded. I ran a five minute mile.

There may have been roses along the way. If so, I missed them.

September 9. Here the preparations for the race end—2.2 miles. Much slower this morning, and much stiffer too, with lots of time to greet school children. Say a slow prayer. See sunflowers.

A silver curtain glitters in the morning sun. It is the back window of the funeral coach, newly waxed and empty, resting on the sidewalk at Mobil. Today I'd like to rest my sore body in the back. I limp around the coach and look back to see if it's Ed Ryan's or Harold Hoare's. No name.

Then I coast downhill to the Key Bank corner, where five retarded men get off the bus and start across the street toward work at Monarch Industries. They have bright new lunch boxes too. Must be the season. Make a mental note to bake butterfly cookies for the children.

I do a re-run past Jenny Herron's Shop, just to make a respectable two miles, and up to the pizza barn where I pause to consider Harold Hoare's funeral home on my right, and Ed Ryan's a half mile up on my left. Like a butterfly between death houses, I turn slowly and jog back home.

Jenny Herron spots me going past her shop. She stumbles out of the red car and hurries over. "Stop. You can stop, Sister. Just jump up and down. Harold Hoare just died. They just told me at the Key Bank. It's scary."

This butterfly is for you, Harold.

September 10. Run with a loaf of homemade bread for those who must bury their dead.

September 11. What you make with tired hands in the night, carry with light feet in the morning. I run early with three tins of butterfly cookies, tuck one in my sleeping parents' mailbox, give one to Lu, the school secretary, and thank her for coming to work, and run down to the kindergarten children with the last and biggest box. They hover close as I lift the lid and let loose a swarming rainbow of butterflies, on wing around the sunny room.

Then it's run upstairs where Mass is being offered for my Grandfather Sauro. I find a seat next to an old Italian relative, who greets me on the lips. Sanctus. Sanctus. Sanctus. She prays half Latin, half broken English. "Lift up your

76

hearts," the priest says. "We leap up to the Lord," she replies. Evidently, she's been out jogging too.

As I give the blood of Christ to each person, my eyes drift like a butterfly, over a few blocks to the grapevines and my grandfather under them, telling us stories. About crossing the ocean seven times (twice free), about laying tracks for the Union and Pacific for twenty cents an hour, about marrying Grandma over in the old country and leaving her too soon to fight World War I, about returning with his buddies on a "freelough" and finding my father, then a little boy, trailing doughboys for cigarette butts. When the war was over, they packed Grandma's crocheted tablecloth and Grandpa's victrola with the loudspeaker into a trunk and left the old country for good.

They had a good life together in the new country, and it was a sad day, just before Palm Sunday, when my grandfather buried my grandmother, in a soaked and blackened grave up at Assumption Cemetery. Not too long after that he went to join her. During his wake we all quietly told stories about him, in tribute, and perhaps to honor the old storyteller. During Mass the pastor wove a homily out of the stories of Joe's life. Then the stories stopped as children, grandchildren, and relatives to the third degree shivered in an ice cold January up at Assumption Cemetery.

The American flag was folded and given to the eldest son. Each of us left a single rose on the coffin, and slowly found our way back to Grandpa's warm and well-lighted dining room with the scrubbed linoleum floor and the oversized table around which the family lived.

Then the stories started again, some of the ones Grandpa had told, getting more embellished in each retelling. And some new ones. One son told the story of Grandpa in the tulip bed, how Grandpa had been thinking of joining Grandma and phoned his son to come over immediately with his camera. When the son arrived, Grandpa carried out the statue of the Sacred Heart, set it on a tree stump in the middle of his glorious tulip bed, managed to kneel down, fold his hands in prayer, look devoutly at the Sacred Heart, and command, "Snap." This was the holy card he wanted distributed at his wake.

One daughter loved the story of Grandma and Grandpa dancing the tarantella on their fiftieth wedding anniversary. The daughter dressed Grandma in lace and jewels and crowned her with a new styled wig. Then she called her brothers. Grandma was three hundred pounds and immobile. Four sons lifted her, chair and all, into a van, out again, and into the LeMoyne Manor. At the sound of the tarantella, Grandpa laid aside his cane, Grandma picked up her skirts in two dainty points, and the two of them lightfooted it for ten minutes, round and round the circle of music and clapping.

As they danced, an old friend tossed a coin at their feet. Later he told his story. This same coin had been thrown when Grandma and Grandpa first danced the tarantella, on their wedding day, fifty years ago in the old country. The friend, then a little boy, had picked up the coin and saved it all those years.

When he finished, I told the story of the three plots. Grandpa put great thought into buying the plot up at Assumption Cemetery. It had to be near the gate, so he and Grandma could go for evening walks. Near the gate too, so that all his old cronies could get off the Lyncourt bus, walk conveniently through the gate, and pay him a visit. Location was important. So was size. Grandpa bought three plots, with his in the center. On one side of him he wanted Grandma, on his other side he wanted me, the only one of his progeny unmarried, and, he thought, unprovided for.

It took months to convince him that I had a place in our community cemetery. Then he was not happy because the cemetery was too far away. He kept pointing to all the priests buried with their families in Assumption. Finally, he gave in and said the old cronies could put a bench on the third plot, to make their visits more pleasant.

As we all told stories around the dining room table, my

grandfather grew like a folk hero, large in stature, vivid in color. I loved all the stories. I never dreamed there were so many sides to Grandpa, nor how much he meant to so many different people. But the story of the three plots will always be special to me because in it Grandpa showed how special I was to him. In it he said I love you and want to take care of you. You don't have a husband, so I want to be sure you have a place in your old age, a good place, with Grandma and me.

In a way my grandfather is like the apples he used to slice and dry over the furnace vents. He would give me a slice and tell me to keep it in my mouth, to let the juice flow back in and fill up the shriveled apple. These stories we tell about him are like juice on the tongue, like life flowing back into a dead grandfather.

> "Slice the apples thin," he said.
> "Then spread them in an old pie plate
> on top of an open grate of heat."
> Preserve by shriveling.
> In the drying fire the just are tried.

> Such a small package of dry bones
> we lay under the flag. The stripes
> could sweep up the pile and scatter
> it to the stars. We lower the bone box
> into the snow cold and pray.

> God who made Grandpa of dust once,
> please make him again, the second
> time round being no task at all.
> We leave him here in a deep freeze, sleeping,
> one snow rose for love's keeping.

> "Store the dried apples in a jar
> and eat them for candy in winter.

Slip a slice into your cheek, so,
and the water fills up the dried apple.
One slice will take you to the A&P and back."

So we tell watery stories to fill up a dry grandfather,
and slip the dry body of God in cheek,
all the way to heaven and back.

The Mass is ended now. We have shared the bread and
wine and stories. Take them home in peace.

September 15. Today I jog 2.5 miles in honor of my anniversary. Twenty-five years ago on this day, I left mother and
father, brothers and sister and all things hopefully to follow
Christ.

Take this gift, my Lord, with twenty-five strings attached, all of them pulling in your direction.

Later in the day we gather for Mass in our front room.

At this time, it is customary for someone here to give a
few words of insight and encouragement based on the Gospel chosen for the occasion. And since I am the one who
chose the transfiguration Gospel, you will be thinking—Oh
good, it is because she has something creative to say.

This will be a disappointment. I chose this Gospel, not
because I know what it means, but precisely because I do not
know. The story is filled with mystery and unexplainable
events, much like the story of our lives.

In the center of the strange Gospel stands the bright
cloud, a kind of contradiction really, for how can a cloud be
bright? A cloud is by definition something that hides and
darkens. How can we have bright darkness?

I do not know, but this bright cloud reminds me of the
photographer's darkroom where I bend over in the dark
and, with a little light, try to make negatives into positives.

While I work with the film, I have a sense that God is working with my own dark and light heart.

In the Gospel story, the three disciples looked up and saw only Jesus. Honestly, I have never looked up and seen Jesus. I wonder if anyone has. What happens, I think, is that we look up out of ourselves and see one another, and sometimes sense the presence of God.

But his presence seems subdued, not dazzling. More like a bright cloud, and sometimes a soft word, or faint music, coming out of the cloud.

And this is the soft word I hear—Jesus is compassionate and forgiving, and, most of all, faithful. Abiding.

September 16. The morning after a party, the house reels with the remains. (And the people reel, too.) Flowers bloom on ledges and table hedges. Wrapping paper and ribbons lie in heaps around the couch, making a flower bed, while the gifts laugh and tumble out of boxes and shelves, above, around, and under a stereo upon which whirls Anne Murray, "I'm happy just to dance with you." Not a bad idea, the gifts think, and start dancing through the house. The house has never seen such extravagance, such foods, such wine and music, such gifts with the lavish hands of givers still on them, such a heavy, intoxicating air of candles, incense and roses.

Out on the porch a new puzzle lies incomplete on a cardtable, left there when the eyelids started to lower. The puzzle is itself an extravagant harvest of fruits in baskets— the remains of love multiplied, given, gathered up in twelve baskets to take through the year.

The spirit in the house wakes me early to slip on jogging clothes and run under the street lights to one who could not come last night. I carry her a bud vase with a pink rose unfolding.

Later I run again, in the sparkling sun. But all the beauty is inside, where yellow roses and pink open themselves, too gentle for words or touch or tears.

God bless all our halting steps.

If you should see God face to face before me, hold me in your eyes, your heart, your rose slow unfolding.

September 17. Today the trees toss and turn fitfully in a gale. The sign at Jocko's Shebeen reels, swings on a single hinge between heaven and earth. Take, Lord Jesus, my mean thoughts and kind, this clean of heart white tied tight and this unraveled one, true song and false, myself lovely, lowly, mean, clean, fitful in the night, wayward, heavenward.

September 26. Windstrong with billows. Clouds and shirts balloon in the breeze.

Overhead, the chestnuts rattle in the wind, let loose, let go, let fall. There will be a gathering all.

He could be a musician—trim grey suit with wide lapels, ruffled shirt, large bow tie, man making his way with halting step up the side entrance of Beebe the dentist. He could be violinist, dentist, patient, one who must play this day with lame foot. Bless all our halting steps.

September 28. Today, the day of the United Way race, we run the car to Boston to do a good turn. Later in the day I jog up and down the ocean.

October 2. I swing open the front room curtains to check the weather. And I peer into the cold steel eye of day.

In the house across the street a curtain hangs in shreds, a ghost in the eye of the window. A hundred thousand leaves are flying north against their will.

After running, I peel off the rainstorm sticking in the soaked jogging clothes. Then it's light the lamp and bake the bread against the dark.

By mid morning the storm subsides and a cable TV truck pulls into the window of heaven and earth. A black man, long of leg, climbs the telephone pole, stiffly, straps himself to, tips his yellow helmet back and takes one look at his new surroundings, takes one long last drag on his smoke, and flips it. He waits resignedly in the eye of the window, strung halfway up between heaven and earth, waits like a patient child strapped to its mother's back, waits, it may be supposed, for his companion to come out of the customer's house.

But the wait grows long, the man grows weary. He climbs back down to earth, stiffly, slips into the truck and waits it out on cushioned seats.

After all, who can wait for long, dangling between heaven and earth? And feet are made for earth, do not climb heavenward easily, not on slick pegs stuck in a pole.

Today is the feast of holy angels. Soft they fly, and easily, on feathered wings, up the pole, across the wires and into the stormy cloud, taking the man in the yellow helmet with them.

October 4.

Virginia Defio
and
Gordon Babo

joyfully invite you
to sing their wedding Mass

this 4th day of October, 1980

With post nasal drip and a voice prone to crack, I run an extra mile this morning, taking great gulps of godly air. Make clean my heart and crystal my mouth. Make me your Voice, singing in a wilderness of love's enduring.

84

October 5. Up early and already packed, the screeching geese are taking their noisy leave, like disgruntled guests. They make no bones about it. There's cold in the air. Time to fly south. No sky of blue or leaf of green beguiles them. Fair weather friends.

Up in the hills the apple farmer also checks the flight of geese, checks the apples still to be picked, checks his wife who is slowly checking and closing the house. The farmer dreams of stretching his limbs in the nice warm sands of Florida. "You should go too. Wait until you get your heat bill."

Instead, we buy his squash and apples and prepare to sing our way through winter.

October 8. The geese still screech across the thick white sky. Their mass evacuation is disconcerting.

During the night I dreamed the house was being evacuated while I slept. First they took down the window of heaven and earth. Then they rolled beds piled high with the house turned inside out, down the hill and into the night.

It was a foolish fright, a child's fear of being left in other people's flight. Now I see it's only the geese leaving. Someone must stay to run on the streets the name of Jesus without end, for the ragtag family coming slowly uphill, the old woman behind them counting her money, and the men on the screeching machines at Lipe-Rollway.

October 9. The killer frost came in the night, laying white death on the face of fruit and flower.

October 16. Outside the window of heaven and earth there grows the tree of the knowledge of joy and sorrow. So close to the house are the branches and leaves that it is difficult to say whether the window nestles in the tree or the tree grows in the front room of the house.

As for brilliance and intensity of color, today the tree rivals the stained glass border of the window.

It is, as I have said, the tree of the knowledge of joy and sorrow, framed in the window of heaven and earth. I plant my feet firmly in the earthly part of the window and stretch for all I'm worth up to the heavenly part.

Today I am distracted by a scene going on in the golden boughs. A man named Zacchaeus sits like a bird in a nest. Zacchaeus is a short man, but straddling the branches he has a perfect bird's-eye view of the sidewalk beneath the tree. He is, indeed, high, and very light of heart, because today Jesus of Nazareth is coming by this very tree, the tree of the knowledge of joy and sorrow.

I stop stretching to watch in the window of heaven and earth.

Down on the sidewalk under the tree waits another man, a tall imposing Pharisee. He also has a perfect view of the walk and plants himself square in the way of the approaching Jesus of Nazareth.

Of course, the unpredictable Christ looks up into the golden boughs and shouts through the camouflage, "Come down here, Zacchaeus. I want to stay at your house." The little man nearly loses his precarious balance and tumbles out of the tree for joy.

Then the Pharisee speaks. "It is not allowed. This man is a sinner." Brilliant head, soul of lead.

And there, in the very presence of Jesus Christ, in what should really be a matter between the two of them, Zacchaeus is forced to defend himself. And finds a ring of sorrow around his joy.

Down at the base of the tree the killjoy voice continues.

"They do not keep the commandments. You are not allowed to eat and drink with them."

"It is Sunday and you are not allowed to stand up, walk and carry that mat around."

"She is a woman of the streets. Her tears and kisses are certainly not allowed."

"You are not allowed to cure the blind man. It is Sunday. You can cure the eyes and withered hand, stop the bleeding, shuck the corn, forgive sins on Monday."

The voice comes like the killer frost, always during some healing touch of God in other people's lives. This is the knowledge of joy and sorrow, learned in the window of heaven and earth. I think of these things as I stretch in the window, sweating to make room in my narrow self.

October 18. There is no escaping the hearse, even at the mother house, this rainy Saturday morning. I'm running the circle, soaked, when the solemn carriage creeps up and parks its prominence at the door. The black caddy is close behind.

> Ring around the rosy,
> A pocketful of posy.
> Ashes, ashes,
> We all fall down.

I pick up speed, shouting, "Rage, oh rage, all you people in the house, rage against the dying of the light. Do not go gentle into that good night. See the trees, soaked to the bone, raging in red and gold. They do not go gentle into that good night. Rage, rage, against the dying of the light."

October 20. There's Halloween in the windows, life size skeletons dancing in the doorways.

October 21.

> Autumn Leaves
> or
> Seven Ways of Looking at the Change

1

The stem and veins of the leaves are blood red,
like so many thermometers, registering dead.

2

The leaves have a toasted look.
They change from the edges in.
Watch the fringe.

3

First the tree begins to smoke.
Then the leaves catch fire from the sun.
Come see the burning tree.

4

While you were gone, green turned to gold.
It will not hold.

5

Quick to cry.
Slow to dry.

6

"That's pretty stupid,"
said the young fellow,
to the woman running
with the yellow umbrella.

7

Oh, no! Please don't go.
Stay, until I get a picture in my eye.
Good-bye.

October 24. Not a hint of wind. Only sun, blue sky, early morning and still. Suddenly, as if on cue, the leaves start coming down, one by one, then in bunches, like golden angels fallen from the sky silently. And their number is legion. They catch the sun as they come, catch hold of one another on the way down so that two fall together, steadily, like gold shower.

It cannot last. I hurry and dress, lace my shoes and run through every tree fall, leaf pile I can find, run zigzag through the world parish like the first woman alive, catching gold angels as they fall, hit and dance off this Joan in soft armor.

Leaves and runaway geese, bless the Lord.

Frost on the grass like broken glass, bless the Lord.

October 25. LSD means long, slow distance. Slowing down a little, I run my best week, averaging 3.7 miles a day.

October 30. Followed by my worst week, no jogging. Working in a cold house, I got cold feet and the flu. Now, flat on my back, I say the Jesus Prayer like an old lady, incoherent, whose guts rise and fall on their own, saying the prayer without her.

November 1. Today I am Elizabeth Barrett Browning on a sickbed. I lie here thinking of my favorite saints and what they taught me.

St. Joy. One month before she was to move out, St. Joy papered her bedroom walls in lovely blue flowers. **MAKE YOUR WORLD BEAUTIFUL TODAY.**

St. Rachel. At the age of fifty-eight, St. Rachel flung her Ph.D. in French to the winds and opened a community care service for the aging. **THE OLDER YOU ARE, THE BETTER THE LEAP FROM STAR TO STAR.**

Robert of St. Libera. Also called the Curé of Ars, for his easy way with the strays. What he received in the left hand, he gave away with the right. His hands were faster than the eye. **WHAT YOU GET IN THE MORNING, GIVE AWAY BE-FORE NOON.**

St. Flannery. **THE GOOD NEWS OF GOD'S KINGDOM IS THAT PEOPLE OF EVERY SORT ARE FORCING THEIR WAY IN.**

November 4. Still sick, I feel like the last woman alive. Old. Enfeebled. Wrapped in an afghan, wrapped in soft drugs, wondering vaguely whose jogging shoes these are.

Some other woman's from a long time ago. You can read her story in this book, if you have the energy.

Maybe in a while I will. When I'm done listening to the wind. Done staring at the four walls, the chairs, the water mark on the table.

But it's important not to sink back into the soft cloud. You must make a move. Walk, before your legs forget how. Exercise yourself like a hostage, for the day of deliverance.

It's easier to sink back into the walls and chairs and water mark.

Finally, I drag on my jogging clothes and walk to the polling place. On the way I am embarrassed. Agnes Gibbons and her cane are going faster than I. Today it takes as much to walk three blocks as it did to run three miles.

November 10. Overhead, squirrels in the attic run frantic, setting up house for a long winter's night.

I put on Barbra Streisand and prepare my comeback, stretching to the soft rise and rolls. I've got the inadvertent shakes.

November 12. The first run back is hardest of all. After two blocks, my breath goes. There's a protesting wheeze coming out of my squeezing lungs. All I can say is "mercy."

90

In my absence, the world put on a somber look. The leaves are gone, stuffed in body bags and propped on curbs. A new President was elected. A truck exploded at the Terpening Company, sending one man in pieces into the rafters. Jenny Herron's window is dressed for Christmas. Next door a baby girl was born.

November 18. The first snowfall is six inches and still coming.

The higher you lift the knees, the faster you go. To strengthen the muscles that lift the legs, run in high snow. Running in the resisting elements like this also improves your balance.

November 19. Standing foot stretch.

In your bare feet, approach the wall and stand there, with your hands at the level of your heart. Keep your feet parallel to each other, six inches apart. Touching the wall with your hands, push up on your toes and down, up and down fifteen times. Then up. And hold.

> In loving you I stand still
> as an angel on the head of a pin,
> more still than angel
> since I am none, but still
> must stand on the head of a pin.

November 21. At Tops Market. 8 P.M.

> And what do you teach, Sister?
> I write books.
> You don't teach?
> I write books.
> What kind of books?

On the spiritual life, and books on how to write books. You've got it easy.

You're into book writing?

I'm into religion. I see you out there every morning, jogging, one of those modern nuns. Well, listen to this. If you really want to know about prayer, stop in at my mother's. Any hour of the day. She says the rosary non-stop. Join her for one. Do you good.

From dawn to dusk I plow the paper, laying out neat rows, until a field full be planted. At the Angelus I pause, a bent peasant up to my elbows in muck.

November 28. We sit around the dining room table for Janet's birthday Mass. Day lowers in the window of heaven and earth. The priest lifts a basket of bread and a cup of wine. My body. My blood. He lowers the meal to the table, to the very spot on the table where hours before the typewriter lay. The table sags with sacrament.

December 1. Better a short run than none at all. Run for the air and the prayer.

December 4. Every parish has one. Some are blessed with two or three. The local idiot, the parish crazy. In the neighboring parish she stands on the pew and yells "Hypocrite!" at the young priest lifting the Host, yells "You're all hypocrites" at the solemn row of communicants snaking its way forward.

At the downtown cathedral, the resident stigmatic groans before the crucifix, clutches and wrenches out a passion play in center aisle. Over to the side a gentle idiot climbs the pedestal and hugs the Blessed Mother in tireless embrace.

We have one too, a parish crazy. He happens to be a childhood playmate of mine. Now he offers the Mass with the priest, bowing, lifting, gesturing, first anticipating a move, then lagging behind. Word has it his mother thwarted a latent vocation. After Mass he presses Padre Pio prayer cards and Louis DeMontfort pamphlets into our hands. But for me he has special attentions.

He slaps me on the back, nudges me in the pew, gives me the handshake of peace and the wink of all knowing. It's that wink I find disconcerting, conjuring up close encounters in the small frozen igloos we made in winter, the blanket tents we hung up in summer, the secret meetings under his front porch.

But isn't that all in the past? Not for the crazy. He knows no passage of time. He is forever thirteen, and I am eternally eleven.

This morning he stands in the snow outside the Twin Trees Restaurant. He waits in the cold for the Centro bus, waits in the season of Christmas for someone to turn on the lights.

December 5. Snowy. All the bushes are fat back lambs waiting for the Lord.

December 8. The Immaculate Conception.

Under the sign for Exotic Dancers, the hooker stands in frozen makeup. Her eyes are permanently violated. A half block up, her sister walks with a bag of laundry slung over her shoulder, walks in clown red lips, painted large, smeared, unsmiling.

"Hi. How are you?"

"Fine. And you?"

"Good."

In San Salvador four sisters are raped, shot, and piled in a common grave. I hear my sisters crying under the sign for

93

exotic dancers, under all that dirt, under the sign of the savior—el salvador.

December 18. We have no crib set, no miniature Christmas town either, with roofs of snow and shutters red. So I get up early and sit at the back window. Down below, roofs of snow huddle in a kind of valley, all the way to the surrounding hills and up. One by one the lights blink on in kitchens. The chimneys tall send smoke signals, straight up in the cold, straight up to the Lord kind and merciful.

Day breaks without much light. Running the dark edge of the street through six inch high snow is a deadly game. Trucks run the edge too. One fall—that's all.

December 19. After jogging yesterday, I walked five miles with gifts of bread. Today I'm running in a snow squall and loving it, with a bag of flour on one hip and a bag of sugar on the other.

Here's to you, Dancer. And you, Prancer, shivering and quaking on the Bernozzi rooftop. Behind them, Santa's up to his beard in snow.

December 22. "The First Noel" comes up loud through the floorboards. Joe's not home downstairs, but he left his music behind, so I warm up on the floorboard carols.

The streets are slush, the sky grey. A car toots and Angie Morrison waves. Widow Morrison, wedged between son and daughter-in-law, on her way to the daily radiology. The cancer came back for Christmas.

At night Janet and I visit her. On her TV set the nativity scene appears in living color, courtesy of the Lutheran hour. A baby in blue bunting lifts a hand to an unkempt shepherd come to worship. Over on the couch Angie traces a map for

94

us across her chest, the unfathomable journey the radiation machine makes, looking for a star.

December 24. A heavy storm watch is in effect.

At precisely three in the afternoon, the sky turns black, and a great forty mile an hour wind rises up from nowhere and comes swirling down around the houses with a vengeance.

It seems more like Good Friday than Christmas Eve. Your entering our world is just as violent an upheaval as your leaving it.

We keep a heavy night watch for you, in the window of heaven and earth.

December 25. COLDEST CHRISTMAS ON RECORD IN CENTRAL NEW YORK.

All the windows are frosted blind in 22° below zero. Outside, morning is frozen stiff, dangerous and beautiful. A bright mist from some other world drifts in the air, circles the snowy trees and hangs suspended over the empty streets.

> Rise up in splendor. Your light has come. The glory
>   of God shines upon you.
> Yesterday, darkness covered you, and thick clouds.
>   But today, the Lord shines on you and warms the
>   frozen places.
> Open your eyes and look around you.

All the fat backed lambs are laughing. I run through wonderland with my eyes frozen open. Many will not make it to church today.

After jogging, I run to the Panuntos with the body of Christ. No red and green in their house. Not much sign of

Christmas at all save two old people waiting for the Lord Jesus. Michael and Antoinette. Their names might just as well be Simeon and Anna.

She is loud and spontaneous in praise, sings "Gloria in excelsis Deo," in Latin, from beginning to end. I sing along as best I can, while Michael nods and smiles against the snowy window, a Christmas shepherd leaning on his cane.

Afterward, Antoinette gives me a shot of anisette and I lightfoot it home.

December 26. Christmas is never like the scenes on the cards we have taped up around our doorways. Neither was the first one—picture perfect.

Your coming is always other than what I expect. And so much more.

I treasure these imperfect pictures, and ponder them in my heart.

December 28. Sometimes it's better to run than fight. Joseph is running today, taking the child and his mother to Egypt.

December 29. No jogging today. I'm riding the bus instead, taking my sinus, laryngitis to the doctor.

You begin to notice things, after you get yourself settled in your seat on the bus, things you don't see when you're jogging. You notice how the new Christmas hats and jackets are off the store racks and onto the heads and backs of people. You notice how some old ladies will not push in. They sit immovable in the aisle seats, mountainous and formidable like the woman across the aisle on my right, or propped and peerless like the woman in front of me. She is small and chicken boned, turned in toward her empty half and unmoving. I found a seat behind her, next to an over-flowing man.

All the stalwart ladies get off in the environs of the Skyline Apartments.

Then you really begin to notice. I say "really" because a small, beat up looking woman, maybe 35, with no new clothes on her back and dirty hands goes suddenly, in the front seat of the bus, into an epileptic fit.

All her joints shoot straight out and freeze. Some hidden motor bounces her up and down the seat violently. She bangs every part, slides down, rolls her eyes so the whites look green and spits green through clenched teeth.

It may be one second or thirty before I stop staring and find myself holding her, putting myself between her and the floor. The motor is big enough for two.

Suddenly, it stops. "Get her shoulders and lift her back up into the seat." A tall, stringy schoolboy does. I wipe her mouth, then her sweating face. She is stunned. Her eyes are blind. Then she starts heaving again. Shorter this time. Then it's over. Except she doesn't know who she is, where she lives, what she's doing on the Centro bus. She wears no identification. No medicine in her pockets, only a single bus token. She lets me hold her arm and rub her back. She shrugs. I shrug back. The wait for the ambulance is endless.

"We could carry her over to St. Joseph's from here. Would be quicker."

"Better yet, drive the bus over."

But we wait. She tries to lift up the bus seat. She looks behind the seat for something she lost. Gloves? Glasses? Everyone's trying to help. She pulls a box of bubble bath out of a small brown bag. Next, she pulls a box of feminine douche out and shows it to me—all four sides of the box. She shrugs. I shrug back, and she goes back to lifting up the bus seat.

When three medics arrive with the ambulance, I go back to my seat and the overflow. He has rescued my mittens from the floor. I sit and wonder if the epileptic spent Christmas with the Salvation Army. Before she gets into the ambulance, she turns and looks at all of us in the bus. As if she misses us. I'm so sorry I have no gift of miracles.

December 30. I'm still thinking of her as I jog today.

The DPW is out early, dumping salt by the truckloads into the streets. My running shoes are salted. So are the feet inside, salted as a newborn babe, in the old rite of baptism. Preserved for life eternal. Keep us all, Lord Jesus.

December 31. There ought to be a gathering, here at the edge of the year. Let there be a coming together before we go home.

Let there come Norcott, Herron and Vanelli. Bonville, Bottrill, Libera, Jakubowski and Ryan. Let there come clown and thief. Painter, pilgrim, dancer, baker, runner, lawyer, doctor and priest. Maker of music, dresses and mayhem. Tender of bars and buses, schools, machines, hearts and houses. The fat lady—brother and sister, mother and father to me. Come.

Let us bring flowers, leaves and trees. Bread and butterflies. Snowballs. The four seasons. Birds, dogs and bandits. Let us call in the angels and saints to say—this is how we lived. This is how we cooked our meals, ate, slept, played, fought, worshiped God, and took care of each other.

O God, sway those considerate scales of yours. Forgive us. Bless us. We are lightweights, with the stones taken out of our hearts, here at the edge of the year.

The arms of Jesus stretch east and west, gathering together the farthest reaches of the sea past and future. Jesus is himself a thin spine bridge to run over, to God our Father.

Each of us is a bridge testifying I am of this place, of this time, of this people, worshiping this God. I do my best. Take what is helpful.